Frommer's®

MEMORABLE WALKS IN ROME

1st Edition

by Bruce Murphy and Alessandra de Rosa

WILEY

Wiley Publishing, Inc.

Published by:
WILEY PUBLISHING, INC.
111 River St.
Hoboken, NJ 07030-5774

ISBN-13: 978-0-471-75651-4
ISBN-10: 0-471-75651-2

Editor: Tim Ryan and Naomi Black
Production Editor: Heather Wilcox
Cartographer: Anton Crane
Photo Editor: Richard Fox
Production by Wiley Indianapolis Composition Services

Front cover photo: Imperial Ruins, Arch of Septimius Severus, Rome.

For information on our other products and services or to obtain techni-
cal support, please contact our Customer Care Department within the
U.S. at 800/762-2974, outside the U.S. at 317/572-3993 or fax
317/572-4002.

Wiley also publishes its books in a variety of electronic formats. Some
content that appears in print may not be available in electronic formats.

Manufactured in the United States of America

5 4 3 2 1

Contents

LIST OF MAPS

The Walking Tours

● ● ● ● ● ● ● ● ● ● ● ● ● ● ● ●

About the Authors

Bruce Murphy has lived and worked in New York City, Boston, Chicago, Dublin, Rome, and Sicily. His work has appeared in magazines ranging from *Cruising World* to *Critical Inquiry*. In addition to guidebooks, he has published fiction, poetry, and criticism, most recently the *Encyclopedia of Murder and Mystery* (St. Martin's Press).

Alessandra de Rosa was born in Rome and has lived and worked in Rome, Paris, and New York City. She did her first cross-Europe trip at age 2, from Rome to London by car. She has continued in that line ever since, exploring three out of five continents so far. Her beloved Italy remains her preferred destination and this is where she lives for part of the year.

An Invitation to the Reader

In researching this book, we discovered many wonderful places—hotels, restaurants, shops, and more. We're sure you'll find others. Please tell us about them, so we can share the information with your fellow travelers in upcoming editions. If you were disappointed with a recommendation, we'd love to know that, too. Please write to:

Frommer's Memorable Walks in Rome, 1st Edition
Wiley Publishing, Inc.
111 River St. • Hoboken, NJ 07030-5774

An Additional Note

Please be advised that travel information is subject to change at any time—and this is especially true of prices. We therefore suggest that you write or call ahead for confirmation when making your travel plans. The authors, editors, and publisher cannot be held responsible for the experiences of readers while traveling. Your safety is important to us, however, so we encourage you to stay alert and be aware of your surroundings. Keep a close eye on cameras, purses, and wallets, all favorite targets of thieves and pickpockets.

Frommers.com

Now that you have the guidebook to a great trip, visit our website at **www.frommers.com** for travel information on more than 3,000 destinations. With features updated regularly, we give you instant access to the most current trip-planning information available. At Frommers.com, you'll also find the best prices on airfares, accommodations, and car rentals—and you can even book travel online through our travel booking partners. At Frommers.com, you'll also find the following:

- Online updates to our most popular guidebooks
- Vacation sweepstakes and contest giveaways
- Newsletter highlighting the hottest travel trends
- Online travel message boards with featured travel discussions

Introducing the Eternal City

A beacon of civilization during antiquity, when it was quite literally the center of the world, Rome's amazing history also includes more than 1,000 years as the spiritual heart of the West, from the Middle Ages through the Renaissance. No other city has played such a defining role in the life of a civilization—really, more than one—for so long. And during those centuries, successive generations of artists and the noble Roman families that were their patrons have lavished artworks on the Eternal City.

Rome today continues to live multiple lives under multiple identities. As the seat of the Vatican, it is still looked to by a billion Catholics as their spiritual home. Its political importance may have shrunk in comparison with the era when it was the cosmopolitan center of the huge Roman Empire—encompassing the whole Mediterranean and stretching north all the way to Scotland and east to the fringes of Indian and Chinese empires. But Rome is still the capital city of Italy, and remains one of the major cultural and art centers of Europe. All roads still lead to Rome for visitors, artists, and pilgrims all over the world.

Introducing the Eternal City

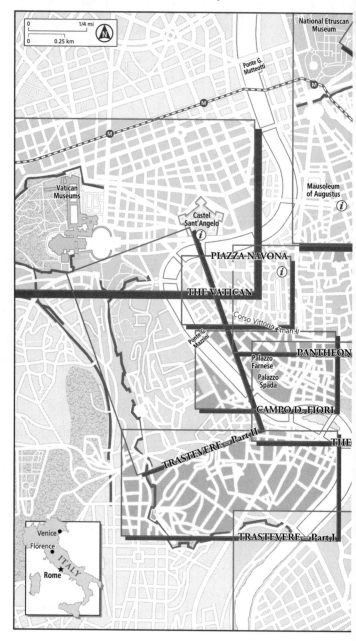

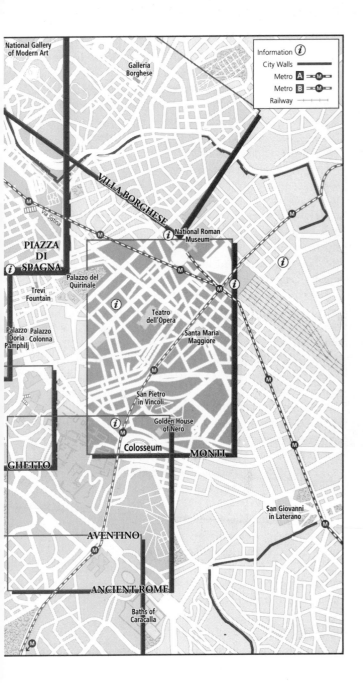

National Gallery
of Modern Art

Galleria
Borghese

Information *i*
City Walls
Metro A ==M==
Metro B ==M==
Railway ++++

VILLA BORGHESE

Via Sistina

National Roman
Museum

PIAZZA
DI
SPAGNA

Palazzo del
Quirinale

Trevi
Fountain

Teatro
dell'Opera

Palazzo Palazzo
Doria Colonna
Pamphilj

Santa Maria
Maggiore

San Pietro
in Vincoli

Golden House
of Nero

GHETTO

Colosseum

MONTI

San Giovanni
in Laterano

AVENTINO

ANCIENT ROME

Baths of
Caracalla

3

The architecture of Rome has evolved right along with its history, from the imposing marble-clad monuments of antiquity to the richly decorated palaces and churches of the Renaissance. Interestingly, the area covered by Imperial Rome was larger than during the beginning of the Renaissance, and it is only with the 19th century that Rome "filled up" its walls again and resumed the proportions it had in antiquity, when it was a city of about two million people. Eventually, with the reunification of Italy and the designation of Rome as the capital of the new state, the city expanded beyond what had been the ancient Roman walls. The remains of the ancient city loom under the modern one, as many of its ancient buildings, roads, and even sewage systems were put to use in later times. Important ancient Roman monuments and buildings poke through the modern urban fabric as a reminder of the ever-present cultural heritage.

In this small compendium of walks we want to guide you not just past the major monuments, but through the Rome that is known only to the real Romans, those who have been living and using those streets since, well, the Romans. We have divided the walks by neighborhood, and each will take you to a historic area where the layering of culture goes back uninterruptedly from contemporary Rome to the ancient city; you will discover that the connecting links of successive generations has never been broken, as seen in the fact that legends and anecdotes linked to this or that stone are still alive today after 1 or 2 millennia.

Rome presents a magnificent face to all its visitors, but its true magic is revealed only to those who take the time to walk its smaller streets. Each of our itineraries will take you near important monuments, which you are welcome—indeed, encouraged—to stop and visit; but our focus is the other Rome, the one that lies undiscovered to most tourist eyes, even though it's often literally just around the corner from the famous sights. All the itineraries are moderate walks, designed to be accessible to all both in terms of physical strain and interest.

ANTIQUITY

Starting from the fortified administrative center on the Capitoline Hill—the Campidoglio, where archaeological excavations have actually confirmed the "foundation" of a city around the legendary date of 753 B.C.—and the residential area on the Palatine Hill, the city developed around the Roman Forum, its commercial and political heart. During the imperial period, the area of the Forum was enlarged with the construction of additional markets and public buildings—the other forums known as the Fori Imperiali—while the whole Palatine Hill was overspread by the emperors' palaces. During his reign, Nero moved his residence to the much-criticized (at the time) Domus Aurea, or "Golden House"—a sort of amusement park for the emperor, of enormous size and lavishly decorated and landscaped (not to mention ruinously expensive). Starting with Vespasian in A.D. 69, the Flavians reclaimed that area and built the greatest of Roman amphitheaters—the Colosseum—and huge thermal baths—the Terme di Tito. In the meantime, Rome had expanded well beyond its initial set of walls.

During antiquity, Rome was a marvel of monuments and imposing buildings dressed in travertine marble, but—with the exception of Nero's house—the purpose of the buildings was purely practical, always to satisfy a need: public administrative buildings, roads, bridges, theaters, public baths. Private buildings were of course also elegant and richly decorated, but always much smaller in scope.

THE BYZANTINE & MEDIEVAL PERIOD

Although today it is hard to find traces of these ages in the urban fabric of the city, this was a momentous period. It saw, above all, the establishment of the power of the church and the beginning, arising out of the ashes and destruction of the barbarian invasions, of the "Rome of the Popes." The Byzantines liberated Rome from the Goths in A.D. 552, and traces of their domination can be found in a number of churches in Rome. However, most Byzantine religious structures were erased by later interventions of the popes, who decided to transform Rome into the capital of western Christendom that it later became. (Doctrinal differences caused the Roman church to devalue the Byzantine tradition.) During this period, many ancient Roman buildings and temples were recycled as churches and as administrative offices, while other areas were completely abandoned. The population had dramatically dwindled because of wars and natural catastrophes—earthquakes and flooding—and the

Black Death. In A.D. 609, Rome had only about 35,000 inhab-
itants, and nearly 1,000 years later, in 1526, it still had only
about 55,000. The area within the perimeter of the ancient walls
was only loosely occupied, with great abandoned islands
reclaimed by vegetation (hence the famous stories of sheep and
cattle grazing in the Forum). It is only during the Renaissance
that these spaces started to be used again.

THE RENAISSANCE & BAROQUE

With the establishment of the papacy as a recognized (and in
some sense ultimate) temporal power in the 8th century and its
increasing role in the battles for power in Europe among the
various royal families, Rome became completely dominated by
the popes and their families, who were constantly embroiled in
their own internal struggle for political influence. Luckily, part
of the battle was played out on artistic and urban grounds, with
the greatest artists being called to decorate churches, build new
palaces, and remodel neighborhoods for the greater glory of
their patrons. Some of these interventions consciously aimed at
deleting previous cultural influences—the Byzantine, for
instance—and at reviving what was increasingly considered
humanity's greatest artistic achievement: antiquity. With some
irony, these great admirers of antiquity settled down to imitate
the grandeur of their predecessors by dismantling their greatest
surviving monuments and using them as building blocks, so to
speak, for their own creations. The popes' aim was to establish
Rome's influence over the world as the spiritual, political, and
religious center; to do so, they needed a scenic background of
grandeur to match. They expended vast resources and wealth to
bring this about. Rome indeed became splendid, but much was
lost in the process.

ROME AS CAPITAL OF ITALY

The popes have not been the only agents in the destruction of
Rome's early postantiquity period; in a tradition that was
already ongoing during the Roman Empire, buildings and
monuments are constantly redecorated, enlarged, rebuilt. The
popes are certainly responsible for a large part of the transformations—especially during the late Renaissance and baroque,
when most of Rome's churches were redecorated and many
buildings and new streets and squares were opened. But in

their turn, the new governments that took power over the city after the reunification of Italy in 1870 set about to undo much of what the popes had done. They felt the need—not only practical but also political—to redesign the city, answering the challenge of transforming the popes' city into a modern capital for a new country. There is actually a surprising continuity in the remodeling plan that was put together by the royal government in the 19th century and that which the Fascists—and then, later, the new Republican government—pursued 100 years later.

ROME IN THE NEW MILLENNIUM

Approaching its 4th millennium, Rome has entered a phase of valorization of the past and intelligent conservation of its existing structures. The destructive approaches to modernization are not only impossible now; much effort has been put into undoing earlier damage. While the first results of this new approach, dating from the 1990s, have definitely brought about some positive changes—the center of the city has been extensively restored and the pedestrian areas expanded—Rome still faces enormous challenges. With a soaring population and an urban sprawl that has devoured the famous Roman countryside with miles of ugly developments and projects, the heart of the city appears besieged. Will the century-old structures of the city center collapse? Will the public transportation system keep up with the increasing pressure? Will the Eternal City collapse under its own weight?

A DATELINE OF ROME'S DEVELOPMENT

1500 B.C.	First settling of villages on the seven historical hills overlooking a fording of the river Tiber.
ca. 753 B.C.	Rome is officially founded by Romulus who, according to legend, traces its square perimeter on the Capitoline Hill. Reality roughly matches myth, with the first traces of an organized town dating from this time, with its administrative and political center on the Campidoglio.

509 B.C.	The grandiose temple of Jupiter is completed on the Campidoglio. In the meantime Rome has been surrounded by a first set of walls.
456 B.C.	The Aventine Hill is designated as the residential area of the plebeians.
390 B.C.	The town is sacked by the Gauls. A new set of walls is put under construction.
142 B.C.	The *Pons Aemilius,* the first stone bridge over the Tiber (today the *ponte rotto,* "broken bridge") is completed.
80 B.C.	Rome numbers about 400,000 inhabitants.
27 B.C.	Beginning of the reign of Octavian Augustus, first Roman emperor, and the Pax Romana ("Roman peace"); this period of security will last until A.D. 180—year of the death of Marcus Aurelius—and corresponds to the maximum expansion of the city.
27 B.C.	First building of the Pantheon.
A.D. 80	The Flavian Amphitheater, later known as the Colosseum, is inaugurated by Titus.
A.D. 118	Hadrian starts rebuilding the Pantheon; in 123 he will start on his own mausoleum— today the Castel Sant'Angelo. Rome's population is estimated over one million.
A.D. 217	The Baths of Caracalla are completed and opened to the public.
A.D. 271	Aureliano starts a new—and larger—set of city walls.
A.D. 326	Pope Sylvester I inaugurates the first St. Peter's Basilica. Emperor Constantine had granted Christians freedom in 313; in 390 pagan cults are forbidden in Rome.
A.D. 395	The Roman Empire splits into the eastern empire with capital in Constantinople, and the western one based at Rome. However, the western capital is moved to Ravenna in 402.

A.D. 410	Rome is sacked by the Visigoths.
A.D. 455	The Vandals sack Rome.
A.D. 476	Western Roman empire brought to an end by Odoacer, king of the Goths. Justinian, emperor of Constantinople and the eastern Roman empire, starts a war against the Goths.
A.D. 552	Occupation of Rome by Narsete, general of Justinian. The Byzantines start to rule Rome and work toward establishing the city as the capital of the western Catholic Church.
A.D. 609	The Pantheon is transformed into a church. The population of Rome has dwindled to about 35,000.
A.D. 756	In the famous "donation of Pepin," the Carolingian ruler (predecessor of Charlemagne) Pepin III recognizes the pope's right to his own state and territory, in exchange for being crowned king of what will be known as the Holy Roman Empire by the pope. The Vatican State has formally begun.
ca. 1200	The Jewish population begins to be transferred into the Rione Sant'Angelo, later to become the Ghetto.
1309	Pope Clement V abandons Rome for Avignon, France; Gregory XI will return to Rome in 1377.
1475	Ponte Sisto, the only bridge built after antiquity and before the 19th century, is completed.
1506	Construction of the new St. Peter's Basilica begins.
1517	Opening of Via Leonina (today Via di Ripetta), the first of the *Tridente* (the Trident), the scenic set of three streets radiating from Piazza del Popolo. It will be completed in

	1543 with the construction of Via Clementina (today, the Via del Babuino).
1526	First reliable census: Rome has 55,000 inhabitants.
1555	Pope Paul IV establishes the Ghetto in the area of the Circus Flaminius. Roman Jews will be obliged to reside there until 1870.
1626	The new St. Peter's Basilica is completed; the colonnade will not be finished until 1667.
1703	The Ripetta harbor on the Tiber is rebuilt.
1726	Completion of the Spanish Steps.
1762	Pope Clement XIII inaugurates the Trevi Fountain.
1800	The city's population reaches 150,000 at this year's census.
1871	Rome is proclaimed capital of Italy after having been occupied by Victor Emanuel II's troops the previous year. The new government begins an ambitious plan to redesign the city.
1874	Termini Station, the new train station, is completed; beginning of the development of the area of Prati (meaning "fields").
1876	The building of new stone banks or ramparts for the Tiber begins, along with the *lungotevere*—the streets along the river.
1885	Placing of the first stone of the monument to Vittorio Emanuele II, the Vittoriano.
1901	Rome's population reaches 422,411 inhabitants.
1926–32	The Teatro Marcello and the Area Sacra dell'Argentina are "liberated"—the existing medieval and Renaissance structures are destroyed and removed.

1933	Opening of the Via dell'Impero (today Via dei Fori Imperiali). In 1936 demolitions for the opening of Via della Conciliazione begin.
1943	Heavy bombardments of Rome by the Allies; the city is placed under German occupation. The deportation of the Roman Jewish community to Germany.
1944	The Germans randomly select and kill 335 civilians as a punishment for a partisan attack on their officers. Rome is liberated by the Allies on June 4.
1950	The new Termini station is inaugurated, together with the new Via della Conciliazione. Rome reaches over 1.5 million inhabitants.
1980	Opening of the first subway line, Metro A.
1995	Beginning of a great restoration and renovation campaign in preparation for the millennium celebrations and the Papal Jubilee of 2000.

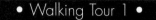

Ancient Rome

Start: Colosseo Metro station.

Finish: Circo Massimo Metro station.

Time: 2½ to 3 hours not including visits.

Best Time: Early mornings and late afternoons, to enjoy the best light.

Worst Time: Lunch recess (12:30–4:30pm), when most of the churches are closed (the Capitoline Museums are closed on Mon and the Domus Aurea on Tues).

Right at the heart of modern Rome lies the archaeological area of the Fori and the Palatine Hill. In Latin, *fori* is the plural of the word "forum," which refers to the center of town. As the largest city in the empire, Rome had not only one forum but several, which were all additions to the original forum, the Forum Romanum (Roman Forum). The Fori and Palatine Hill were the heart of the ancient city, with its Capitol, its major public buildings, temples, and markets, and (later) the Imperial Palace.

Feeling today like a strange hole in time cut through the urban fabric, the area occupied by the Fori and the Palatine was very much integrated in the life of the city until the 20th century. The area's layered architecture stood as a testament to

Rome's long, rich history. Medieval and Renaissance buildings surrounded, and often were built directly over, ancient Roman temples and structures. While some of the largest monuments such as the Colosseum had been used as a quarry for marble and construction materials by the popes of the Renaissance as they were busy rebuilding the city, other structures remained largely intact because they had been turned over to other uses. Temples were transformed into houses and churches, or used as foundations for newer buildings.

While premodern ages are often blamed for lacking our historical sense and appreciation for the past, the truth is that the Fori and Palatine Hill area suffered as much, if not more, from urban "renewal" in the late 19th and early 20th centuries as it did in the previous thousand years. The kings of the House of Savoy began the damage with the building of the monument to Vittorio Emanuele II over the Campidoglio—a symbolic location, meant to establish the continuity of the postunification monarchy with antiquity. Unfortunately, making this architectural-political statement required the demolition of a large part of the neighborhood that had developed on the hill. The Fascist regime completed the spoilage by demolishing the entire neighborhood that lay between the Colosseum and Piazza Venezia; the government justified this demolition by constructing the Via dei Fori Imperiali, the major thoroughfare now connecting the two landmarks. (It was a high price to pay just to facilitate what today we consider the bane of urban existence—traffic.)

The Fascist government also demolished part of the remaining neighborhood on the Campidoglio to create Via del Teatro Marcello on the western side of the hill. The government also "isolated" all ancient Roman monuments by demolishing whatever later building had been built around and over them, even if these structures were hundreds of years old. It is actually surprising that anything survived and still remains to be seen.

The lost neighborhoods—said to have afforded numerous magical and picturesque views of ancient Roman buildings layered with Medieval and Renaissance additions—are gone forever. However, in an attempt to recover some of the archaeological remains covered up by the Via dei Fori Imperiali, and perhaps to make amends for the scientific loss, an ambitious

Ancient Rome

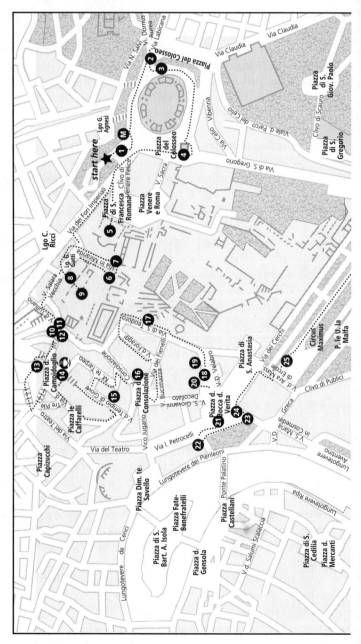

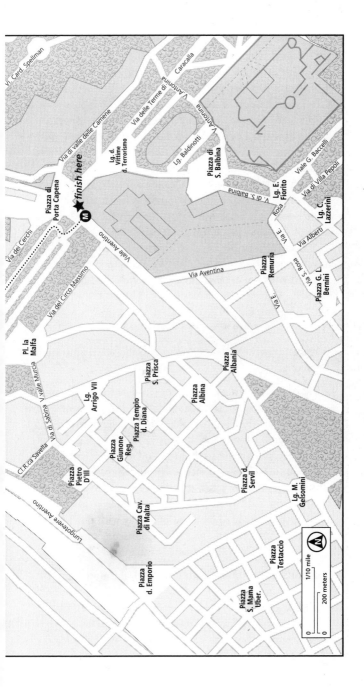

archaeological excavation was started in 1998. This much-criticized project, which is open to the public, focuses on the Imperial Forums (east of the Roman Forum), and is the largest archaeological excavation in the world. At the time of this writing, the work is approaching its final phases. When it is complete, ancient Rome will be more alive than ever to visitors.

The Fori and Palatine Hill are probably the most visited area of Rome, yet few tourists venture into the streets where we'll take you, and even fewer notice the many landmarks that are of such great historical and cultural importance to Romans today. During this walk we show you the grand monuments of ancient Rome, but we also lead you through the tiny leftover corners of the lost neighborhoods of the Campidoglio, so that you can have a glimpse of what the neighborhood was like before the government rebuilt it. We also point out monuments and works of art that are usually overlooked by harried tourists. Explore!

• • • • • • • • • • • • • • • • •

Walk out of the Colosseo Metro stop and you'll find yourself on:

1. **Via dei Fori Imperiali.** This road is the single most criticized urban intervention of the Fascist regime; it erased one of the most picturesque neighborhoods of Renaissance Rome and destroyed much archaeological evidence. Excavations currently underway are creating a system of arched tunnels beneath the Via dei Fori Imperiali that give access to treasures that were paved over during the road's construction (unfortunately, for practical reasons, the road can't be done away with now).

   Turn left, walking past the Colosseum and up the slope of the hill to the entrance of the:

2. **Domus Aurea (the Golden House),** the most grandiose of Nero's follies. The sprawling palace sat in a beautifully landscaped park that occupied the whole valley of the Colosseum and extended to the Palatine Hill. Since Nero had dissipated so much state money (that was real gold decorating his "golden house"), his successors—the emperors Vespasian and his son Tito—had to work hard to restore faith in the government and refurbish the state's finances.

One of their first actions was to dismantle Nero's Domus Aurea and replace it with buildings of public utility: the Colosseum (see below) and great public baths such as the Terme di Tito, remains of which are still visible above the Domus Aurea and in the park behind it. The Domus Aurea is open Wednesday to Monday 9am to 7:45pm; last admission is 1 hour before closing. Admission is charged.

Directly across from the Metro station, just off Via dei Fori Imperial, is the imposing structure of the:

3. **Colosseum,** which was built between A.D. 70 and 80. Ancient Romans referred to the Colosseum as the Flavian Amphitheater because it was a gift from the new Emperor Vespasian (of the Flavian family) to the people. The gift was not completely disinterested, of course; the famous political strategy described by Juvenal as *Panem et Circensis* (literally "bread and circuses") is a formula that still makes complete political sense: People who are well fed and amused are easy to govern. This magnificent building rises four floors above the ground for a height of 50m (164 ft.) and has a diameter of 188m (617 ft.). It took 100,000 cubic m (over 3.5 million cubic ft.) of travertine marble and 300 tons of iron to build. Once completed, the Colosseum could hold more than 50,000 people. During days of intense heat or rain, spectators were protected by a huge tent—called the *velarium*—that was pulled over the top of the arena using a complicated system of ropes and pulleys maneuvered by a crew of sailors. Contrary to popular belief, the amphitheater was never used for the martyrdom of early Christians—they were prosecuted by the Roman government only for individual acts of political insubordination and not as a religious sect—because citizens were given much liberty to worship in religiously eclectic Rome.

Several kinds of games were held in the amphitheater: chariot races, sports competitions, shows of exotic animals, and the extremely popular gladiatorial games. These were bloody and violent affairs in which trained men—mostly war prisoners who fought to earn their freedom, but also professional gladiators who performed for the glory and the money—confronted each other or ferocious beasts in a fight to death.

A Brief History of Rome

As legend has it, Rome was founded by Romolo (Romulus) and his twin brother Remo (Remus). Mars (the god of war) fathered these demigod twins; the mother, the daughter of a local king, Rea Silvia. After a close escape from death—they were saved by a wolf who nursed them—the twins grew up and set about establishing a new town. After a dispute, Romolo took over and marked on the ground the limits of his new town. The date: April 21, 753 B.C. Rome grew to be a beacon of civilization, absorbing and borrowing any good features from all other cultures it encountered (or conquered) and creating a set of rules, principles, and laws that are still the bedrock of modern Western values and institutions.

Rome began as a collection of shepherds' huts populated by the local Italic tribe. The **Etruscans,** a local people famed for their seafaring, gold and metal work, and trading, deeply influenced the town. The Etruscans gave Rome its name, drained the swamps, built sewers, and introduced writing. Weakened by their struggles with the Greeks who were colonizing southern Italy, the Etruscans lost their power over Rome near the beginning of the 5th century B.C.

The **Roman Republic** was founded in 509 B.C., when the last of Rome's kings was overthrown. The republic was headed by two consuls and the senate, all controlled by the upper or *patrician* (aristocratic) class. The *plebeians* (the working class) later obtained their own council and were represented by tribunes. It took hundreds of years for Rome to gain control over the Italian peninsula, including decades of bloody war with Carthage (the Punic Wars, which began in 264 B.C.). The city suffered many reverses.

Gradually, Roman military supremacy was established. When the Carthaginian general Hannibal took 6 months to march over the Alps to attack the Romans from behind in 218 B.C., that marked the start of the Second Punic War. Eventually the Punic Wars ended with the Romans erasing Carthage from the map in 146 B.C. The door was then open for Rome to spread its influence across the Mediterranean. It ruled its provinces through governors and allowed subject countries to retain local government and customs—though betrayal of Rome was brutally avenged. The Republic became fantastically rich, and Hellenic and Eastern art, wealth, and cultural influences flowed into Rome. Recent archaeological finds show a Roman presence as far away as China's borders.

Caesar became a tyrant after his defeat of **Pompey**—this marked the beginning of the Roman Empire. Following Caesar's murder on the Ides of March (Mar 15) in 44 B.C., civil war ensued. Caesar's grandnephew and adopted son, Octavian, won and became the first emperor, **Caesar Augustus.** His regime turned Rome into a glowing marble city we think of. A string of mostly debauched and even insane rulers followed: **Tiberius, Caligula, Claudius,** and **Nero.** Rome famously burned in A.D. 64 under Nero's reign (though not, perhaps, by his own hand).

The last hurrah, so to speak, for the Roman Empire came in the 2nd century, when it enjoyed a string of "good" emperors who brought order, stable succession, and civility to the empire: **Nerva, Trajan, Hadrian, Antoninus Pius,** and the philosopher-emperor **Marcus Aurelius.** With the ascension of Marcus's 19-year-old son, **Commodus** (the villain of the fictionalized film *Gladiator*), the empire was headed once again for trouble. With his assassination in A.D. 192, the empire plunged once more into chaos.

When **Emperor Constantine** converted to Christianity and founded Constantinople in A.D. 330, Rome's wealth shifted east. The western empire began to crumble under barbarian pressure: The **Goths** sacked Rome in A.D. 410; the Huns came next under **Attila,** and they were followed by the **Vandals** of North Africa. In A.D. 476, the German chief Odoacer deposed the western Roman emperor, in effect signaling the end of the once invincible Roman Empire.

How did the Flavian Amphitheater become known as the Colosseum? After the famous fire of 64, Nero constructed a colossal gold statue of himself, represented as the sun god, with his head surrounded by rays. The emperor Hadrian moved the statue of Nero to the area adjacent to the amphitheater. In medieval times, people started referring to the amphitheater as the "Colosseo," the place of the *Colossum,* or enormous statue. The spot where the statue once stood is marked today by a platform planted with cypresses.

Transformed into a fortress during the Middle Ages, the edifice was donated to the city in the 14th century. The popes used it as a quarry for building materials. The holes in its walls are the casings for iron clamps that attached the travertine marble that originally covered the building. The marble was removed for reuse in other buildings, such as St. Peter's Basilica. In the late Middle Ages, the Colosseum was believed to be the gate of hell and a meeting ground for the spirits of all the gladiators and slaves killed there. To augment its dark fame and the local ghost population, the nearby Esquiline Hill was largely occupied by cemeteries and places of communal burial, where bodies of criminals and the homeless were easily disposed of.

You can visit this monument daily from 9am to 1 hour before sunset (last admission is 1 hr. before closing). Ticket price includes admission to the Palatine Hill.

Just southwest of the Colosseum is Rome's most famous triumphal arch, the:

4. **Arch of Constantine,** built by the Roman Senate in A.D. 315 to celebrate the victory of Emperor Constantine over Massenzio in A.D. 312. If you are surprised by the speed of construction, you might be interested to know that the Romans "recycled" a number of statues and relief sculptures taken from earlier monuments, such as the statues of barbarian prisoners at the top of the four columns on each facade, and the medallions over the lateral arches on both facades. The end product, though, is indeed magnificent—the largest and the best conserved of ancient Rome, second only to the Arch of Trajan in Benevento.

Walk back to Via dei Fori Imperiali and immediately to your left (on the side of the street opposite the Metro) climb the Clivo di Venere Felice. This leads to the church of:

5. **Santa Francesca Romana.** Built in the 9th century, this church was enlarged in the 10th century and named Santa Maria Nova in contrast to Santa Maria Antiqua (see below). In the 12th century the elegant Romanesque bell tower was added, which you can still see today. The church's name was changed again in the 15th century, in honor of Santa Francesca Romana, who pronounced her vows here in 1425. The facade and the interior decoration date from the 17th century, but inside are many earlier works of art. One of the most intriguing is the basalt slabs protected by a metal grating on the wall of the right transept; these are the *Silices Apostolici,* bearing St. Peter's imprint.

The painting over the main altar is a 12th-century Madonna with child, and the mosaics of the apse date from the same period. Several other very early master-pieces decorate the crypt, including a precious icon from the 5th century that belonged to Santa Maria Antiqua.

Walk down the ramp and turn left on Via dei Fori Imperiali. Walk north to Largo Romolo e Remo. Climb the ramp to the left of the archaeological area of the Roman Forum and turn left on Via in Miranda. Located here is the entrance to the church of:

6. **San Lorenzo in Miranda.** This church was built in the 7th to 8th century inside part of the temple of Antonino and Faustina (the front of the temple can be viewed from inside the archaeological area of the Roman Forum). The main altar and the painting of St. Lawrence's martyrdom above it are both by Pietro da Cortona. In the first chapel to the left you'll find a *Madonna with Child and Saints* by Domenichino, who also designed the chapel's decorations.

Also on Via in Miranda (across from San Lorenzo in Miranda) is the new facade of the basilica of:

7. **Santi Cosma e Damiano.** This church was built in the 6th century inside the public library of the Foro della Pace—a forum built by Vespasian in A.D. 71 to 75—and one of the halls of the Temple of Romulus, a temple facing the Via Sacra inside the archaeological area of the

Roman Forum. The church was remodeled in the 17th century, when its floor was elevated by 7m (23 ft.) to bring it to the level of the Campo Vaccino (the pasture that had covered the Roman Forum), transforming the new lower level into a sort of crypt. The new facade and entrance date from 1947, but don't let that fool you; inside there is still much of value to see.

In the hall to the left of the entrance you can still see the original pavement of the ancient Foro della Pace; from the entrance you access the 17th-century cloister where there are doors to both the church and the crypt. The apse of the main church—strangely shortened by the elevation of the floor in the 17th century—is decorated with the original 6th-century mosaics and a painting of the Madonna with child from the 13th century (over the main altar). In the lower church you can see the original 6th-century floor and altar.

Walk back down to Largo Romolo e Remo and turn left; here you will find the entrance to the archaeological area of:

8. **The Roman Forum.** This was the center of public life in ancient Rome. The Forum developed as early as the 7th century B.C., when the existing marshes were drained through the construction of the Cloaca Maxima, which conveyed the water to the Tiber. Building the forum was a natural step in Rome's development because the marshy area is situated on a straight line that originates in the very early settlements on the fords of the Tiber River near the Tiberina island, connects the two adjacent market areas—the Foro Boario and the Foro Olitorio (see Piazza della Bocca della Verità, later in this chapter, and chapter 6, "The Ghetto")—and ends at the Roman Forum. Most of Rome's economic, political, administrative, and religious activities were held in the buildings of the Roman Forum, which eventually stretched from the Capitoline Hill on one side to the Palatine hill on the other.

Because it was completely abandoned with the fall of the Roman Empire, much of the Roman Forum was progressively buried under centuries of sediment and reclaimed by vegetation. In medieval times it was called Campo Vaccino (cow field) and used as a pasture. During

The Palatine Hill (Palatino)

This hill was the residential area for noble families from the foundation of the city back in the 8th century B.C.; it became the seat of the Imperial Palace with the ascension of Augustus (Rome's first emperor) in the 1st century B.C. So definite was the hill's vocation as residence of Roman nobles that its Latin name—*Palatium*—is the word we still use today for such housing: palace. In a corner of the hill (west of the House of Augustus and southwest of the House of Livia) is the *Casa Romuli,* a hut that was celebrated during antiquity as Romulus's house and restored.

The Palatine is also where the most ancient rituals were celebrated, including the festival of the goddess Pales on the 21st of April—the day of the mythical foundation of Rome, which is still celebrated today—and the *Lupercalia,* the festivals held by the grotto at the foot of the hill where the she-wolf is said to have raised the mythical twins Romulus and Remus. A real wolf was kept there until the late 1960s—I remember seeing it as a child and being duly impressed by the thing, but more than a bit sorry for the wolf, which looked truly sad in those dreary surroundings with heavy traffic noise and smoke.

The Palatine was abandoned at the end of antiquity but rediscovered in the 16th century by the powerful Farnese family, which built a grandiose villa there, the famous Orti Farnesiani, of which little can still be seen. Indeed, after the family was extinguished, the villa was progressively torn down in order to proceed with the archaeological excavations that began in earnest in the 18th century. Only part of the villa's magnificent gardens remains today.

A visit of the Palatine Hill is very rewarding for both the many remains of the Imperial Palace and the famous frescoes of the Casa di Livia, but also for the evocative atmosphere and views over Rome. It is open daily 9am to 1 hour before sunset and there is an admission fee, which also includes the Colosseum (see above); we definitely recommend a guided tour, for which you can sign up at the archaeological office (☎ **06/39967700**).

the Renaissance it became a source of construction materials free for the taking. It kept an important role in the life of the neighborhood, though. For example, it was the site of the traditional confrontation that was carried out once a year, pitting the youth of Trastevere against the youth of the Rione Monti (the neighborhood of the Imperial Fori east of the Roman Forum). This was very much a contact sport; the *sassaiola* (throwing of stones) was a real battle, with opponents wearing leather and steel body armor, and injured victims left on the ground. The best feats of courage were then celebrated in the local *osterie* on the evening of the battle, with plenty of wine to help.

Excavated and transformed into an enclosed archaeological park in the late 19th century, the area has been recently reopened to free public access (daily 9am to 1 hr. before sunset). If you plan on fully exploring this site, we definitely recommend that you book an official guided tour to make it all come to life (call the archaeological office to sign up for one at ✆ **06/39967700**).

Enter the archaeological area of the Roman Forum. Walk straight from the entrance, cross the Via Sacra, and you will come to the church of:

9. **Santa Maria Antiqua.** Still under restoration at press time, this church was built using some of the lower halls of the Imperial Palace on the Palatine Hill and consecrated to St. Mary in the 6th century A.D. It is decorated with splendid frescoes and has an interesting history. After the church sustained earthquake damage in the 9th century, it was abandoned in favor of the new church Santa Maria Nova (today called Santa Francesca Romana; see above). In the 13th century, Santa Maria Liberatrice was built over the ruins of Santa Maria Antiqua to celebrate Pope St. Sylvester's victory over a dragon. Legend has it that the beast—which had killed many innocents with its poisonous breath—dwelled under the nearby temple of Castor and Pollux, and that the pope confronted it armed only with a crucifix. Tamed by the pope's invocation of the Virgin, the dragon meekly followed him away from the temple.

Santa Maria Liberatrice was demolished in 1900 to free and restore the older church beneath. Santa Maria Antiqua is due to be opened to the public again soon.

Walk out of the archaeological area again and turn left on Via Salara Vecchia toward the:

10. **Capitoline Hill (Capitolino).** Strategically situated, this hill had two summits: The *arx,* to the northwest, was home to the temple of Juno Moneta and the first mint of ancient Rome; and the *Capitolium,* to the southeast, where the monumental temple of Jupiter—later dedicated to the Capitoline Triad of Jupiter, Juno, and Minerva—was originally built in the 6th century B.C. (this temple was destroyed in a fire in 83 B.C.). In A.D. 78, the elegant building of the Tabularium—the state archives—was built between the two summits, dramatically walling off that end of the Roman Forum.

In Roman times, there were only two ways to access the hill. First was the Clivus Capitolinus, climbing up from the Via Sacra in the Forum. Second was two ramps of steps: the *Scalae Gemoniae* connecting the Forum to the *arx,* and the *Centum Gradus* connecting the Campus Martius to the Capitolium and passing by the Tarpeian rock (see below).

Abandoned in medieval times, the hill became the Monte Caprino (Goat Mountain), used for animal pasture. The only inhabited building was the monastery and church of Santa Maria in Aracoeli (see below). The hill regained a bit of its public functions with the building of the Palazzo Senatorio over the Roman Tabularium (see Piazza del Campidoglio later), and its slopes became alive with houses and convents. All this medieval warren of structures was then destroyed with the construction of the monument to Vittorio Emanuele II and of the Via del Teatro Marcello shortly after.

Take Via del Tulliano to your left and after a short climb you'll come to a belvedere overlooking the Forum, where you'll find the church of:

11. **Santi Luca e Martina.** Originally built in the 7th century inside part of the Forum of Caesar, it was completely rebuilt between 1635 and 1664 by Pietro da Cortona. The

luminous interior is one of his masterpieces, but the exterior is surprising since the church was isolated by the demolition of adjacent buildings in preparation for construction of the Via dei Fori Imperiali. The artist obtained the right to have his family tomb inside the church, and you can see his burial monument on the floor of the upper church. He also designed the beautiful altar of Santa Martina in the lower church.

Opposite the church is a portico giving access to the:

12. **Carcere Mamertino.** This building housed the state prison from the beginning of Rome. In the 17th century, a church was built over the original building, which can be visited underneath. While its facade dates from 40 B.C., the building is older; you enter into a square room where, from an opening in the floor, you can gain access to the circular room below; this is where the prisoners were thrown (and where they were eventually strangled). Legend has it that this was the prison where Saint Peter was held and that on that occasion he baptized his guards with the water from the underground spring existing there, but there is no historical proof. You can visit daily from 9am to 5pm in winter and from 9am to 6:30pm in summer. No admission is charged but offerings are welcome.

Continue past the church and climb the ramp of stairs to your right to Via di San Pietro in Carcere; follow this straight for a few steps and then turn right up another ramp. This leads to the **portico** of the monastery attached to Santa Maria in Aracoeli (see below). It is all that remains of the monastery, which was demolished together with the spectacular belvedere tower nearby, for the construction of the monument to Vittorio Emanuele. Before the portico to your left are the two remaining floors of the Romanesque bell tower and the lateral entrance of:

13. **Santa Maria in Aracoeli.** Here you will find yourself in the right nave of the church. Santa Maria in Aracoeli was originally a Greek monastery built in the 7th century over the remains of the temple of Juno. In the 13th century the church was completely rebuilt; the exterior and the cosmatesque (a mosaic of marble and colored stones)

floor inside are original and date from that period. The naves are divided by antique marble columns, while the coffered ceiling is from the 16th century. The interior contains frescoes of various periods, including a whole cycle by Pinturicchio in the first chapel from the main entrance to the right, depicting the life of San Bernardino. There are also frescoes by Benozzo Gozzoli in the third chapel on the left from the main entrance. Among the artwork, also notice in the right transept the 13th-century tomb of Luca Savelli, one of sculptor Arnolfo di Cambio's masterpieces.

Exit the church from its main portal and descend the steep set of stairs leading to Piazza Aracoeli. Notice to your right the Romanesque bell tower of the small church of **San Biagio de Mercato;** this was built in the 11th century over an *insula* (ancient Roman residential block) from the 1st century—one of the few examples remaining of this kind of architecture, which was the typical dwelling of ancient Roman plebeians. Originally, the insula was probably six stories high; four stories are still visible.

Turn left and climb the monumental staircase designed by Michelangelo (the staircase was even more dramatic before being shortened in the 1920s for the opening of the Via del Teatro Marcello). Notice the two lions, which are original Egyptian sculptures from the Roman temple of Isis; they were transformed into fountains in the 16th century and placed here. Notice also the huge blocks in the garden to your right, which are the remains of the walls of Republican Rome, dating from the 7th century B.C. At the top of the staircase is:

14. **Piazza del Campidoglio,** perhaps Rome's most beautiful square, and well worth the climb. It was designed by Michelangelo, together with the facades of the surrounding buildings, and finished after his death. To your right is the Palazzo dei Conservatori, probably built in the 12th century, with the new facade designed by Michelangelo in the 16th century. To your left is the Palazzo Nuovo, built in the 17th century following Michelangelo's design for the Palazzo dei Conservatori. In front of you is the Palazzo Senatorio, built in medieval times over the Tabularium

(Roman State Archives) but also with a new facade based on Michelangelo's design. The piazza is surrounded by a balustrade decorated with antique artwork. The two statues of the Dioscuri with their horses date from the late imperial age, while the remains of two colossal statues of Constantine and his son Constantius II are from the thermal bath of Constantine. The glorious statue of Marcus Aurelius on horseback (set on a pedestal designed by Michelangelo) is a copy; the original was moved inside the Capitoline Museum in 1981. The unique pavement design of the square was built in 1940, but was carefully constructed following an original drawing from 1567.

The palaces house the Capitoline Museums, which include a picture gallery, beautifully decorated halls, and extensive collections of antiquities. Here is conserved, for example, the famous **lupa capitolina,** a 5th-century B.C. bronze sculpture of the she-wolf that nursed the mythical twins Romulus and Remus. From the museums you can also visit the Tabularium. This imposing building stood over 11 great arches and housed the archives of the Roman Empire, including civil registries. In the Middle Ages, the building was used as a deposit for salt and as a prison. You can visit the museums Tuesday to Sunday from 9am to 8pm (last admission is 1 hr. before closing). There is an admission fee.

Take a Break In the terrace of the Palazzo dei Conservatori is a great cafe and restaurant where you can comfortably sit and enjoy the views. They provide several levels of service in elegant surroundings. The place is quite popular for an *aperitivo,* especially in fair weather.

Walk to the right of the Palazzo Senatorio and descend to the **belvedere,** from which you can admire the most beautiful view over the Roman Forum and the Colosseum. It is spectacular at sunrise but also very atmospheric at night. Another great view is from the left side of the Palazzo Senatorio, from where you can also see some remains of the medieval buildings that were taken down in the 20th century.

Next take the Via delle Tre Pile, to the right of the Palazzo dei Conservatori; this is the most remote part of the hill and rarely visited. Here was the house of Michelangelo, which was demolished in the 19th century (the facade was rebuilt in 1941 on the Passeggiata del Gianicolo). Passing the 16th-century monumental portal, which leads to the Villa Caffarelli, you'll see to your left at number 1 **Palazzo Clementino,** built for Pope Clement X in the 17th century; at number 3 stands **Palazzo Caffarelli,** built in the 16th century over the ruins of the temple of Jupiter. Remains of the temple still stand in the little garden to the left of the entrance to Palazzo Caffarelli, while the panoramic terrace across the street from the palace rests on some of the temple's supports.

Continuing on, you reach Via di Villa Caffarelli; turn left at the end onto Via del Tempio di Giove, lined to your left with 19th-century buildings, and to your right by the Belvedere Tarpeo. This was built over the famous:

15. **Tarpeian Rock (Rupe Tarpea),** where starting from a very early period in Rome's history, criminals and traitors were thrown to their death. Used until quite late in the Roman Empire, it was a place of capital executions again until the middle of the 16th century. The tradition started when Rome was only a citadel on the Capitoline Hill, strenuously fighting against the Sabines. The historian Titus Livius reports that in the 8th century B.C. Tarpeia, the daughter of the gatekeeper, let the king of the Sabines Tito Tazio and his men into the citadel in exchange for "what they had on their left arm." She had in mind the heavy gold jewelry the Sabines wore but instead she was crushed by the heavy shields they also carried on that arm, and then thrown from the high rock. From that time forward, a free-fall from the rock became the traditional punishment for traitors.

Continuing straight past the belvedere, enter the vaulted passage under an 18th-century building; it leads to an elegant 16th-century **portico** designed by Vignola. The staircase at the end of the passage leads back to Piazza del Campidoglio. Instead, retrace your steps out of the portico and turn left to continue on Via del Tempio di Giove.

Turn right on Via del Monte Tarpeo, which runs at the bottom of the Tarpeian Rock and turn right on Via della Consolazione. You'll arrive at Piazza della Consolazione, the location of:

16. **Santa Maria della Consolazione,** a church built in the 15th century together with the building behind it—originally a hospital—and completely redone in the 16th century. It is richly decorated with frescoes and paintings by important artists, including Antoniazzo Romano and Giovanni Baglione.

Cross the piazza and turn left into Via San Giovanni Decollato, leading into one of the few surviving corners of the neighborhood demolished in the 1920s. Turn left onto Via Bucimazza and stroll down it to Via dei Fienili, getting the feeling of what this whole area must have been like. Follow Via dei Fienili to Piazza della Consolazione and, retracing your steps, back to Via Bucimazza. Here, turn left into Via dei Foraggi and stroll to the end.

Turn right onto Via del Foro Romano and immediately right again on Via di San Teodoro. Here on your left you'll see the church of:

17. **San Teodoro,** built in the 6th century but completely redone in the 15th century. The apse inside is still decorated with the original mosaic from the 6th century.

Continue on Via di San Teodoro and turn right onto Via del Velabro, graced in the middle by the:

18. **Arco di Giano (Arch of Janus Quadrifrons).** This four-faced arch may have been a triumphal arch in Roman times or simply to give shelter to Romans in this once-bustling commercial area. In the Middle Ages it was used as the portal for a fortified tower—the Torre dei Frangipane—which was demolished in the 19th century to restore the Roman monument. Ironically, the "restorers" also took down what they thought was a medieval addition that instead later turned out to be the top of the ancient arch, built of bricks and covered in marble.

Before the arch is the church of:

19. **San Giorgio in Velabro,** with its Romanesque bell tower, another example of a church rebuilt in the 9th century over

an older church (this time dating from the 5th or 6th c.). San Giorgio has had many additions and renovations throughout the centuries; in the 1920s it was restored to its original Romanesque appearance. Inside, the three naves are divided by antique columns and decorated with 13th century frescoes by Pietro Cavallini (restored in the 15th c.).

To the left of the church is the:

20. **Arco degli Argentari,** a monumental Roman arch that was one of the entrances to the Foro Boario (animal market) that occupied the whole Piazza della Bocca della Verità (see below). Built in 204 by the *argentarii* (money-changers), it is dedicated to emperor Septimius Severus, his wife, Julia Domna, and his sons, Caracalla and Geta. All of them are represented in the inner face of the arch—notice that the figure to the left was abraded: It represented Geta, the younger son who was murdered in 211. The death of Severus the year before had left the boys (Caracalla was 22, Geta 21) in charge as coemperors, a recipe for trouble. Caracalla had Geta assassinated and afterward ordered all his younger brother's images and inscriptions destroyed.

A few steps away, at number 3 of Via del Velabro, you can get a glimpse of the **Cloaca Maxima,** the main channel that drained the water from the Forum and conveyed it to the Tiber. Built in the 2nd century B.C., it is still in use—you can still see it coming out just south of the Ponte Palatino, behind the temples of Piazza della Bocca della Verità (see below).

Continue descending Via del Velabro to:

21. **Piazza della Bocca della Verità.** This large square corresponds to the **Foro Boario,** Ancient Rome's animal market. Located by the ford on the Tiber, this marketplace—together with the nearby Foro Olitorio (see the Ghetto walk)—was in use since the Iron Age. Across from you are two temples that were "isolated" by the demolitions of 1924–25. The round one is commonly referred to as the **Tempio di Vesta,** because it is circular in shape like the Vestal temple inside the Forum; however, it is now believed to be the Temple of Ercole Vincitore, dating from the 2nd century B.C. It is the oldest surviving building in Rome, and was transformed into a church in the

12th century—its roof, believed to be a cupola, was lost. The second temple is commonly called the **Temple of the Fortuna Virile,** but it was actually a temple to Portunus, the god protecting the nearby harbor on the river; it was also transformed into a church in the 9th century.

Walk north and take Via Petroselli; immediately to your left at number 54 you will find the:

22. **Casa dei Crescenzi,** one of Rome's few preserved and complete medieval buildings. It was built between 1040 and 1065 by Nicolò di Crescenzio to protect the nearby ford on the Tiber and was restored in 1940. It is interesting to see how different pieces from antique buildings were reused in the construction.

Retrace your steps to Piazza della Bocca della Verità. Across from the temples and among the trees you can see a 13th-century palace—the **casa dei Pierleoni**—which has been heavily remodeled and renovated in later periods; to its right is the church of:

23. **Santa Maria in Cosmedin,** one of the oldest in Rome. It was built in the 6th century over two previous structures: a 3rd-century chapel and the ancient Ara Maxima of Hercules (Great Altar of Hercules) from the 5th century B.C., which is still visible in the church's crypt. Santa Maria in Cosmedin was enlarged in the 8th century and splendidly decorated (*cosmedin* means "ornament"). It is one of the few Roman examples of Byzantine and medieval art.

Outside the church you can admire the seven-story Romanesque bell tower from the 12th century and, under the portico, the famous:

24. **Bocca della Verità (Mouth of Truth).** This round carved marble disc was an ancient version of what we would call a manhole cover, originally placed over an aperture of the city's drainage system (the carving depicts a river god). It was placed here in the 17th century. Legend wants us to believe, however, that this stone did much more than guard a drainage pipe. It is said that if you tell a lie while putting your hand inside the face's mouth, it will chop it off. Accordingly, it became a test for

proving one's sincerity, and in fact the stone was really used in the Middle Ages to punish liars, whose hands were cut off by a man with a sword hidden behind. A witty story less grisly than this truth has become attached to this tradition, and concerns a noble young woman accused by her husband of adultery. She was brought in front of the stone and, as the crowd parted in front of her, a young man rushed forward and kissed her, pretending to offer a last Christian tribute to the poor woman. She walked to the stone and, placing her hand in position, declared that no man but her husband and the youth who had just kissed her had ever touched her. As a result of the ingenious action of her lover (the young man, of course) and her prompt understanding of his cunning plan, she was acquitted.

Retrace your steps and walk right from the church entrance, then turn right up Via dei Cerchi, passing on your left the imposing ruins of the Domus Augustana and on your right, a building that once housed a pasta mill, to the:

25. **Circo Massimo (Circus Maximus).** This grand space was used for many public performances but is most known for its violent chariot races. It measured 650m (2,132 ft.) long by 125m (410 ft.) wide and was many times rebuilt and decorated with statues and two obelisks—one now in Piazza del Popolo and the other in Piazza San Giovanni in Laterano. The circus was expanded by Trajan first and then by Caracalla from 150,000 seats to 350,000. In use until A.D. 549, it was lined with businesses and stores. The medieval tower on the grounds is the **Torre della Moletta,** built in the 12th century by the monks of the nearby monastery of San Gregorio to defend the mill that existed there.

You can walk inside the circus—it is used as a park by Romans—and reach the Metro station Circo Massimo at its other end.

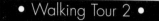
Piazza Navona

Start: Piazza Madama (Bus C3, 116, 116T, 30, 70, 81, 87, 492, and others all stop here, on Corso Rinascimento).

Finish: Piazza Madama.

Time: 2 hours, excluding visits.

Best Time: Mornings Monday through Friday after rush hour is over, and mid- to late afternoons Tuesday through Saturday.

Worst Time: During the hectic morning hour 8am to 9am, Sundays, and the lunch lull when churches are closed to visits.

The neighborhood enclosed between Corso Rinascimento and the Tiber River is the heart of postimperial Rome, with a tight fabric of streets and buildings that trace their origins to the end of the Roman Empire and the beginning of medieval times. Before the opening of Corso Vittorio Emanuele II in the 19th century, Piazza Navona and Campo de' Fiori (see Walking Tour 5) were one neighborhood and together represent the only area of Rome that has been continuously inhabited and highly urbanized since ancient Roman times. This is also the area with the fewest Roman ruins, because in Roman times it was called the Campus Martius or "field of Mars" (Mars being the Roman

Piazza Navona

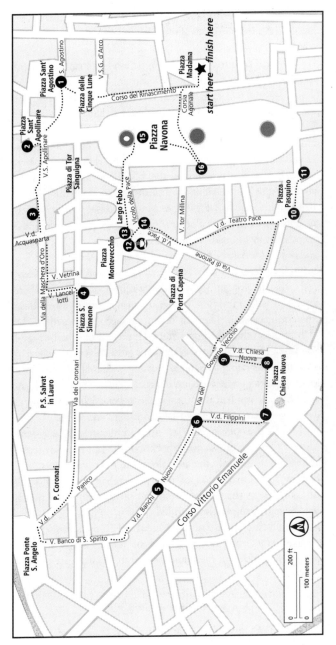

god of war and the origin of our word *martial*). This area was mainly used for military training and was mostly marsh until a drainage canal was built.

The few constructions from those early Roman times were public buildings—such as Domitian's Stadium (Piazza Navona)—and two main streets, the Via Recta connecting the pons Elius (Ponte Sant'Angelo) with the urban section of Via Flaminia (the Via del Corso), and the Via Papalis connecting the same bridge with the Forum. Renamed and rebuilt during the Renaissance, these thoroughfares still exist today for us to explore.

Urbanization started after the fall of the Roman Empire, when most of Rome's population clustered here along the Tiber—the Goth invaders had cut the aqueducts, and hence the river was the only source of water. Further development occurred along the major pilgrimage roads to the Vatican, such as the Via Papalis (today Via dei Banchi Nuovi, Via del Governo Vecchio, and Via di San Pantaleo). In the 14th century, this was the only area within the ancient Roman city walls that was truly urban; everywhere else, fields held primacy over built-up areas (a dream for modern environmentalists!). The real boom, though, happened in the 15th century when the popes started a process of urban renewal that brought about the construction of great palaces and churches, often integrating previously existing medieval buildings (in some ways, the popes were less destructive than 19th-c. nationalists). Elegant residences surrounded smaller enclaves of poorer dwellings, alternating with artisan workshops and stores.

While the opening of Via Vittorio Emanuele II cut off the southern section of this neighborhood, the rest remains virtually untouched. Only the area along the river has been modified by the construction of the new embankments and the Lungotevere at the end of the 19th century, and a few buildings have had more stories added.

You'll find the charm of this part of Rome stronger than perhaps any other neighborhood of the Eternal City, and meandering through these ancient streets is one of its greatest pleasures.

• • • • • • • • • • • • • • •

Lots of buses stop at Piazza Madama, on Corso Rinascimento (see above). More stop along the nearby Corso Vittorio Emanuele II and Largo di Torre Argentina.

Walk north from Piazza Madama along Corso Rinascimento to Piazza delle Cinque Lune; this stretch of the street was opened in 1936 by demolishing a line of Renaissance buildings and moving back the facade of those on the west side of the street. One of these buildings—the **Palazzetto delle Cinque Lune,** an elegant 15th-century palace by Antonia da Sangallo il Giovane, was saved and rebuilt on the piazza that bears its name; you can see it to your left. Turn right on Via Sant'Agostino, passing under the arch, onto:

1. **Piazza Sant'Agostino,** where you find the 15th-century church of the same name, dedicated for use by the Augustinians (the order of St. Augustine of Hippo). The church was renovated by the architect Luigi Vanvitelli in the 18th century and again under Pope Pius IX in 1870. The principal attraction of this church is that Raphael worked here; his portrait of Isaiah can be seen on the third pilaster on the right side of the main nave. Bernini, Sansovino, and other artists have also left their mark on Sant'Agostino over the centuries; Caravaggio's *Madonna of the Pilgrims* is in the first chapel of the left nave.

   Retrace your steps to the Piazza delle Cinque Lune; cross the piazza, and to your right will be Piazza Sant'Apollinare, whose name comes from a medieval palace (Palazzo di Sant'Apollinare) dating from at least the 14th century, when it was turned into a cardinal's residence (it occupies the right-hand side of the square). This is one of the few medieval palaces left in Rome, though it has been restored several times. Attached is the church of the same name; the current incarnation is from the 18th century but there has been a church on this spot since as early as the 7th century.

   On the northwest corner of the square is:

2. **Palazzo Altemps,** which is both one of the great palaces of Rome and one of its best museums. It was closed for many years but has recently reopened. The palace was begun in the late 15th century and incorporated earlier medieval buildings, traces of which can be seen inside. The museum is part of the **Museo Nazionale Romano** (℗ **06/39967700**), which holds some critically

important works of sculpture, particular the Ludovisi collection. The famous *Trono Ludovisi* is a Greek work of bas-relief dating from the 5th century B.C. The *Galata* is an equally renowned statue of a Gaul, apparently committing suicide; a giant sarcophagus depicts battles between Romans and barbarians. Admission is charged.

From the Palazzo Altemps, take Via Sant'Apollinare (to your right). You will quickly find yourself in Piazza di Tor Sanguigna, named for the family of the Sanguigna who had a fortress here; their medieval tower can still be seen rising above a renovated fortress. Also on the square, at **numbers 12A–13,** is a palace that contains the only extant remains of the statue of Domitian that graced the stadium dedicated to the emperor (the stadium is now Piazza Navona). **Number 13** is also the entrance to the **ruins of the stadium of Domitian** lying beneath the square. The ruins can be visited by guided tour but reservations must be made in advance (✆ **06/2412352**).

Cross the Piazza di Tor Sanguigna, which brings you to the small:

3. **Piazza Fiammetta,** which is named for the courtesan Fiammetta who was the lover of the notorious Cesare Borgia. The **casa di Fiammetta** (house of Fiammetta) faces the piazza and dates from the 14th century, though it has been restored over the years. The facade has the arched windows typical of the early Renaissance. From the piazza, turn right onto Via degli Acquasparta, where you can see the side of the house of Fiammetta and its little loggia. There are several other interesting buildings on the Piazza Fiammetta; at number 11 is the 16th-century **Palazzo Olgiati,** and at 11a, the **Palazzo Ruiz** dating from the same period.

Retrace your steps to Piazza Fiammetta and merge right on Via della Maschera d'Oro, which is lined with 15th-century palaces. At number 7 is **Palazzo Milesi,** whose facade gives the street its name: The "maschera d'Oro" (golden mask) refers to the fresco by Polidoro da Caravaggio, much of which has disappeared. Beside the Palazzo Milesi is another 15th-century building with a form of decoration popular in the 1300s and 1400s, called *graffito*. In this style the facade was first painted black and then scratched away, rather like an etching, resulting in a distinctive black-and-white style of painting. Very few examples of *graffito* still exist in Rome.

Turn left on Via Lancellotti, walking along the facade of the 16th century palace of the same name. Then turn right on:

4. **Via dei Coronari.** The name of this street comes from the sellers of sacred objects, particularly rosary beads *(corone sacre),* who did their business with medieval pilgrims traveling to the Vatican (the street was part of the *Via Recta,* which connected the river with the Via Flaminia—today's Via del Corso). Today the Via dei Coronari is known for its almost countless antique shops, selling everything from furniture to tapestries to Old Master paintings.

The street is lined with Renaissance and baroque palaces, among the most notable of which is the building at **numbers 26–28,** the **Palazzetto Diamanti Valentini,** an elegant three-story house. At **number 156–57** is a Renaissance house from the early 15th century that is also called the **casa di Fiammetta** (a sign of Cesare Borgia's largesse, perhaps). Continuing on, you will notice to the left, at the corner of Vicolo Domizio, a shrine that is known as the *Immagine di Ponte.* It was erected by one Alberto Serra da Monteferrato, a Vatican official, in the early 15th century. He has entered the lore of Rome as a result of his lucky escape from the German troops of Charles V during the sack of Rome in 1527; he fled to the nearby fortress of the Castel Sant'Angelo, where he promptly collapsed from a heart attack.

Via dei Coronari ends in Piazza dei Coronari; at the end of the street is the **Palazzo Emo Capodilista** (at numbers 135–143), which is notable for its beautiful *altana* (a terraced structure that sits atop the building and is situated over the exit of the staircase to the roof).

If you turn right here, you come to Ponte Sant'Angelo, the magnificent bridge designed by Bernini (see Walking Tour 8). On this side of the Tiber, it starts from Piazza Sant'Angelo, which was traditionally used for capital executions. Instead of crossing the bridge, turn left on Via del Banco di Santo Spirito (Santo Spirito Bank Street). *Banco* means "desk" and refers to the table that money-changers used to weigh coins and calculate exchange rates; our modern word *bank* is derived from *banco.*

At number 61–60 is the **casa di Bona Dies,** a 15th-century house that incorporates the remains of a medieval portico with granite columns and a carved marble cornice of ancient origin. Continue on, and to the right you will see the **arco dei Banchi,** an ancient arch on which you can see a mark showing how high the Tiber used to flood in this low-lying neighborhood. Rome's oldest plaque is also mounted here; it commemorates the great flood of 1276.

At number 31 is the **Palazzo del Banco di Santo Spirito,** which gives the street its name. This medieval *palazzo* once housed Rome's mint; two of Rome's great architects, Sangallo and Bramante, redid the palace in the 16th century. Its curved facade once matched the piazza in front; however, the construction of the Corso Vittorio Emanuele II in the 19th century cut right through here, ruining the symmetry.

Turn left on:

5. **Via dei Banchi Nuovi (Street of the New Banks).** This is the ancient "Via Papalis," one of the pilgrimage routes to St. Peter's. It still preserves its Renaissance flavor with building after building dating from the 15th and 16th centuries. One of the most famous architects of the period, Carlo Maderno, lived at **number 1–4,** a beautiful Renaissance palazzo.

Via dei Banchi Nuovi ends in:

6. **Piazza dell' Orologio,** which used to be called Piazza di Monte Giordano and is one of Rome's most charming hidden squares. Its newer name comes from the Torre dell' Orologio, a whimsical baroque masterpiece built in 1647–49 and designed by Francesco Borromini. This clock tower alternates concave and convex planes (the front and back of the tower are concave, and the sides are convex) in what some have said is an imitation of the shape of a cog in a clock mechanism. It is crowned by an openwork iron belfry that supports the three bells of the clock.

The clock tower actually belongs to the:

7. **Palazzo dei Filippini,** the "Filippini" being followers of saint Filippo Neri, who founded an oratory here in 1551. The palace is also by Borromini and stands on the site of a 12th century church (torn down to make room for the quarters of Neri's new religious order). The order still exists, so only a portion of the complex is open to visitors. The right-hand side of the building is still used by the order, but the remainder houses various cultural institutions, especially archives and libraries having to do with Rome (including all the newspapers published in the city since the 1700s). The entrance is at number 18 of Piazza della Chiesa Nuova, which you can reach by walking up the short Via dei Filippini. The **oratory** is one of the rooms built by Borromini, a rectangle with the corners rounded off and two loggias on the short sides—one for the cardinals and the other for musicians and singers who would provide music during the recitation of sermons. The **refectory,** which is located between the second and third courtyards, is elliptical in shape. Also worth seeing is the library on the third floor **(Biblioteca Vallicelliana),** for which Borromini designed not only the room but the furnishings—including a gallery accessible through hidden spiral staircases.

To the right-hand side of the entrance to the Palazzo dei Filippini is the:

8. **Chiesa Nuova (New Church),** which once stood on a beautiful square lined with Renaissance palaces. However, as part of the building of the Corso Vittorio Emanuele, the entire southern wing was torn down. It would have matched the concave form of the north side, which was meant to show the church's "embrace" of the communicants. The Chiesa Nuova occupies the site of Santa Maria in Vallicella (Our Lady in the Little Valley), which was given to Filippo Neri in 1575 by Pope Gregory XIII when he formally recognized the order. The design of the church was begun by Matteo da Citta di Castello and finished by Martino Longhi il Vecchio; its late Renaissance appearance can be distinguished from the more baroque style of the Palazzo dei Filippini, which was constructed

later. The interior of the church is more noteworthy than the exterior; it is decorated with frescoes by Pietro da Cortona, including the *Triumph of the Trinity* in the cupola and the *Assumption of the Virgin* in the apse. In the presbytery, you will find Peter Paul Rubens's *Virgin with Child,* flanked by paintings of saints Domatilla, Gregorio Magno, and others. The sacristy has a statue of Saint Filippo Neri himself, by the great sculptor Algardi. The saint is buried in the sanctuary, which is only open 2 days a year. However, the chapel of St. Filippo Neri (to the left of the presbytery) is a marvel of marble inlay, mother of pearl, and semiprecious stones.

Retrace your steps back to Piazza dell' Orologio; to your right begins:

9. **Via del Governo Vecchio,** which was also part of the pilgrimage road to St. Peter's (the "Via Papalis"). Palaces dating from the 15th to the 17th century line both sides of the street, including, at **number 3,** the **Palazzo De Sangro,** with monumental portal and balcony, and at **number 123, Palazzetto Turchi,** built at the end of the 15th century. Greatest of all is the **Palazzo del Governo Vecchio,** at **number 39.** It was built between 1473 and 1477 for Cardinal Stefano Nardini, who became governor of Rome (hence the name of the street). The marble doorway has a frieze of small palm trees over it, and the architrave of the first-floor windows still has the name of the cardinal carved on it. When you enter, notice that the courtyard to the left preserves the original portico and loggia. If you walk around the right-hand side of the palace on Via dei Parione, you can see the facade of the attached **San Tommaso in Parione,** a 12th-century church rebuilt in the 16th century with a facade decorated with carved lion heads. At **number 104,** note the facade of the 13th-century house and its carved marble medallions.

At the end of the Via del Governo Vecchio, you reach:

10. **Piazza Pasquino,** named for the much-mutilated statue that stands at the eastern side. It is a remnant of an ancient Roman copy of a Greek original of the 3rd-century B.C., which depicts Menelaus, a Greek king who

fought in the Trojan war, holding the slain body of Patroclus, the great warrior Achilles' closest companion. The statue was found in Via di Parione (behind you) and set up here in 1501. From there it took on a second career as the most revered of the six "talking statues" of Rome, which acted as ombudsmen, so to speak, for the discontents of the Roman populace. You may see signs hung around the neck of the statue with short satirical verses written on them, usually criticizing whatever government is currently in power. Political tolerance is a relatively recent invention, and during the centuries when the city was ruled by the popes and the nobility, the statues were an indispensable way of anonymously posting criticisms. Legend has it that the name Pasquino comes from a tailor who lived nearby, and who toiled making clothes for prelates who worked at the Vatican from whom he picked up all sorts of gossip and dirt. His tongue, it is said, was as sharp as his scissors and needles, and he couldn't keep these secrets to himself. We derive our word *pasquinade* from Pasquino's satirical jabs.

The statue of Pasquino leans against the corner of:

11. **Palazzo Braschi,** a trapezoidal palace whose main facade faces onto Piazza San Pantaleo (yet another square mutilated by the opening of the Corso Vittorio Emanuele II). Pope Pius VI had the palace built in the 18th century for his family. Their tenure was relatively brief; finally finished in 1811, it passed to the new Italian state in 1871. Today it houses the **Museo di Roma** (© **06/67108316**), which has a collection of painting, sculpture, and objects (furniture, carvings, carriages, ceramics, and even clothing) that illustrate Rome's history and culture from the Middle Ages onward. A permanent exhibition memorializes artwork, buildings, and even neighborhoods of Rome that have disappeared. The main staircase is decorated with 18 red granite columns that originally were part of the emperor Caligula's portico. A lengthy restoration and reorganization of the palace and museum was completed in 2005 (admission is charged).

From Piazza Pasquino, take the Via del Teatro Pace; cross Via di Tor Millina, then bear right into Via della

Pace. You will notice that the building on the right-hand side has had a corner sliced off (during the baroque period) in order to create a better vista as you look toward the:

12. **Piazza di Santa Maria della Pace,** named for the church of **Santa Maria della Pace (Our Lady of Peace).** This extremely important church was closed for many years but is open once again. A church (S. Andrea de Aquarizariis) already stood on this site, perhaps since medieval times, and was rebuilt in 1482. The convex baroque facade, designed by Pietro da Cortona and added in 1656, influenced many artists, including the great painter, sculptor, and architect Giovanni Lorenzo Bernini (see St. Peter's Basilica in Walking Tour 8, and Piazza Navona below). Inside, however, the form of the earlier church was not disturbed.

This church is off the beaten track, but its truly astounding artwork makes it well worth the visit. The first chapel to the right, the Chigi chapel, was decorated by **Rafael.** His monumental frescoes of the sibyls are somehow squeezed into what is actually a quite small space, giving them a coiled force entirely appropriate to the subject. Other great artists also contributed to the church: The baptism of Christ in the chapel to the right of the altar is by Gentileschi, while the main altar and the statues were designed and executed by Carlo Maderno. The paintings of saints in the arch of the apse are by one of the leading female painters of the age, Lavinia Fontana. On the altar is the Madonna della Pace, which gives its name to the church. Legend has it that when a stone was thrown at it, the image miraculously bled.

☕ **Take a Break** Antico Caffè della Pace. Located in the piazza of the same name, this cafe is one of the most famous of Rome—right up there with Caffè Greco (see Walking Tour 4). At Via della Pace 3, its ivy-covered facade is unmistakable. The wicker outdoor tables are a delightful (if somewhat pricey) place to tarry in the good weather, while the elegant interior has marble-topped tables and bar.

To the left of Santa Maria della Pace is the:

13. **Chiostro di Santa Maria della Pace,** also known as Chiostro del Bramante. This small and perfectly proportioned cloister was designed by Donato Bramante and built in 1500–04; this was, in fact, his first work in Rome (he was originally from the Marches). The portico on the ground level is made up of columns supporting arches, while the second-story loggia has square pilasters that complement the round columns. Amazingly, the cloister has never been altered or reconstructed, which has added to its reputation as an exemplary work of Renaissance harmony and order. The interior rooms of the cloister are often open for exhibitions; if none is showing, you can still gain access to the cloister by ringing at Arco della Pace 5.

    Take the little alley to the right side of Santa Maria della Pace (called Vicolo della Pace), along the side of the church of:

14. **Santa Maria dell' Anima.** This church began as a chapel for the Flemish, Dutch, and German pilgrims to Rome in the Middle Ages, and it remains the German church in Rome to this day. The church faces Via Santa Maria dell' Anima, but access is from Piazza Santa Maria della Pace 20. It was rebuilt at the beginning of the 16th century (1500–23). The interior follows the plan of typical German churches, in which the ceilings of the lateral chapels are as tall as the main nave. The paintings inside are of German subjects but mainly by Italian artists.

    The Vicolo della Pace opens to the left into Largo Febo, a pleasant triangular space with a small garden in the middle. Instead of walking through the garden, continue straight into Via dei Lorenesi, which will lead you to:

15. **Piazza Navona.** The oval shape of Piazza Navona reveals its ancient origins as the stadium of Domitian, which was built before A.D. 86 and able to accommodate as many as 30,000 spectators. Situated exactly on the north–south axis, it is 275m long (902 ft.) and 106m wide (348 ft.). Domitian's stadium replaced an even earlier athletic arena made of wood (built by Julius Caesar) and an amphitheater of Nero. In the 8th century, the ruins were used for oratories, and in the later medieval period, houses with towers. In 1477, the market that was

formerly held on the Campidoglio (see Walking Tour 1) was moved here. The brick pavement was laid around this time.

Standing atop the ruins of Domitian's stadium is one of the best-known squares in Rome, a triumph of baroque style. Three fountains punctuate the vast space. The central fountain is the famous **Fountain of Rivers,** designed by Giovanni Lorenzo Bernini and built in 1651. (It was such an artistic triumph that it won over Pope Innocent X, who had originally not been keen on Bernini.) Rising from the enormous basin is a massive rock decorated with a lion, a horse, and sea serpents. The four rivers, depicted in the form of giant mythological figures, are the Nile, the Rio della Plata, the Danube, and the Ganges. At the time Bernini designed and built the fountain, he had a vicious rivalry with the architect Borromini. According to the lore of Rome, two of the figures in Bernini's statue play out this rivalry: The Nile's head is covered in a cloth to avoid looking at the facade of Sant'Agnese in Agone (see below), which was designed by Borromini and sits directly across the piazza from the fountain. (An alternative historical interpretation states the Nile is hooded because the river's source was unknown.) The figure of the Rio della Plata, who also faces Borromini's church, raises his hand in terror as if expecting the facade to collapse.

For his part, Borromini is said to have sided with those who said, during construction, that Bernini had made mistakes in the hydraulics and the fountains would never work. Bernini had the satisfaction of arranging for the water to burst forth just as the pope's cortege passed by.

At the south end of the piazza is the **Fountain of the Moor;** the central figure is depicted wrestling with a dolphin. At the other end of the piazza is the **Fountain of Neptune,** which was actually devoid of figures until 1878, when the sea god and various Nereids and sea horses were added to make it symmetrical with the fountain of the Moor.

On the west side of the piazza facing the fountain of the Moor you will see a large Brazilian flag hanging from the Renaissance **Palazzo Pamphilj** designed by Rainaldi and built in 1644-50. Today it is the seat of the Brazilian embassy. Just to the right of it is the church of:

Summer Fun on Lake Navona

The emperor Caligula once had scores of ships lined up in the Gulf of Baiae, and a bridge built across them, solely for the pleasure of riding his chariot across them. He was not the only ancient Roman who was fond of such outrageous entertainment. Domitian, who ruled in the 1st century A.D., liked to have his stadium (which provided the footprint for the present Piazza Navona) filled with water and used for "naumachiae," or staged naval battles, using scores of vessels and hundreds of combatants. This custom died out with the fall of Roman civilization (the barbarian invaders had cut the aqueducts). But the flooding of the piazza was revived in the 17th century. Just as American city dwellers like to open the fire hydrants on broiling summer days, the nobility of Rome during the Renaissance liked to escape from summer heat by having the Piazza Navona flooded; the outlets of the fountains would be plugged up, and when the water in the piazza had reached sufficient depth, they would then take their usual drive around the piazza in their carriages. Sometimes carriages shaped like boats were built just for this use. The Roman populace would gather to watch, and a carnival-like atmosphere developed, to the point that frolicking and skinny-dipping in the "lake" began to be a common sight. This was considered highly indecent behavior in the Rome of the popes, and eventually punitive measures were taken— and rather extreme ones at that. A sort of sawhorse was prominently erected on the piazza, on which transgressors were publicly whipped or even tortured. Even children were not allowed to frolic in the lake anymore.

Finally, in 1865 the practice of flooding the piazza was permanently abandoned, out of fear—probably not misplaced—that the stagnant waters were adding to the problem of transmissible diseases in the city.

16. **Sant'Agnese in Agone,** which commemorates the martyrdom of Saint Agnes. Tradition holds that she met her death on this spot, which would have been in the arcades of Domitian's stadium (known to have accommodated brothels). It is said the virgin saint was stripped naked, but her hair miraculously grew to cover her body. (Inside, the altarpiece by Alessandro Algardi depicts the miracle.) A church occupied the site as early as the 7th century, but in 1652 Carlo Rainaldi was commissioned to design the current structure by Innocent X. It was greatly modified by Borromini, who changed the facade and added the tall cupola.

Cross the piazza and take the Corsia Agonale, a little street that brings you back to Piazza Madama on Corso Rinascimente.

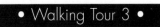

Pantheon

Start: Piazza San Silvestro (bus 52, 53, 61, 71, 80, and 160).

Finish: Piazza San Silvestro.

Time: 2 hours, excluding visits.

Best Time: Mornings Monday through Friday after rush hour is over, and mid- to late afternoons Tuesday through Saturday.

Worst Time: During the hectic morning hour 8am to 9am, Sundays, and the lunch lull when churches are closed to visits.

Thanks to the creation of pedestrian streets in the surrounding area, the Pantheon is a pool of tranquillity amid the hustle and bustle of modern Rome. On all sides, narrow lanes radiate outward, offering picturesque views and numerous attractions (not to mention inexhaustible shopping and eating opportunities). And yet, though the area around the Pantheon is one of the most heavily visited parts of Rome, it is also the political center of the Italian state, with the principal parliamentary and executive offices just around the corner. You'll encounter lots of people but relatively few vehicles: a few electric buses, Lancia limousines, and cabs. On the other hand, you don't have to walk very far before you run into one of Rome's major traffic routes, which do not make for pleasant strolling (hence this itinerary has you spend as little time as possible on them).

The Pantheon, dating from the 1st century B.C., is the most perfectly preserved ancient Roman monument in the world, owing to its later conversion to a Christian church. Other ancient structures in the neighborhood were less lucky. For instance, all but a few traces of the Baths of Agrippa have disappeared, which were the oldest public baths in Rome but fell victim to urban renewal in 1621 when Pope Gregory XV had the last bits demolished. Over the centuries, some of the piers that supported the huge Saepta Julia have been found deep underground. This building was planned by Julius Caesar and served a number of uses—a polling place, site of gladiatorial games and naval battles, and a market bazaar. To the north and east of the Pantheon was the temple of Marcus Aurelius, near the present-day Piazza Colonna (the column depicting his triumphs is still here; see stop 25). Between the Pantheon and Piazza Venezia was a temple to Isis and Serapis, known as the Iseo Campense, built by the emperor Domitian (who ruled A.D. 81–96) but destroyed in the late 1500s. This part of central Rome was densely inhabited throughout the early and later Middle Ages, and buildings from that period have survived, as well as grand palaces erected during the Renaissance. The palace of the Quirinale (on the hill just to the east) was at that time a papal residence, and rich and influential Romans constructed magnificent homes in the area between the Trevi Fountain and the Pantheon to be near the seat of power. This part of Rome has always been a crossroads, where the routes from the north and east met.

Lots of buses stop in the Piazza San Silvestro, and this is a convenient place to start your walk, though the piazza is not in itself much of an attraction (there are shops and the main post office, however).

● ● ● ● ● ● ● ● ● ● ● ● ● ● ● ●

Turn and face the piazza with the post office at your back. Directly ahead of you, Piazza San Silvestro opens into the smaller Piazza San Claudio, which fronts on the busy Via del Tritone. Cross the Via del Tritone (carefully), and take the street a little to your right, the Via Santa Maria in Via, which is named for the church on the corner:

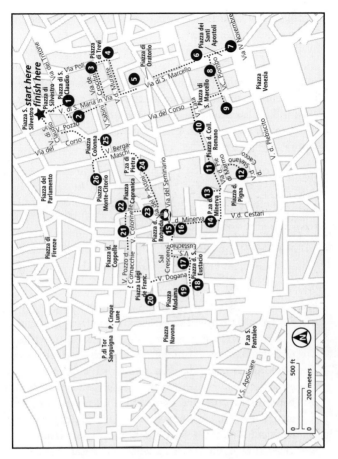

1. **Santa Maria in Via.** This church was built before A.D. 1000, though like most churches in the city it has been renovated many times. It is named for an image of the Madonna that was found, according to legend, in a well on this site (the icon is located inside and to the right of the altar). The church's current facade dates from the baroque period and was designed and executed by two of its masters, Giacomo della Porta and Carlo Rainaldi.

   Walk up the Via Santa Maria in Via. Across the street, to your right, you will see the:

2. **Galleria Colonna,** now referred to as the Galleria Alberto Sordi, after a famous Italian actor. The gallery is

actually a pair of open-air corridors lined with shops, and elegantly appointed with marble and ironwork. Galleries like this one were in a sense the first shopping malls, and were built in other cities, including Naples and Milan, in the late 19th century. The Galleria Colonna has been recently renovated and features chic boutiques and cafes.

Turn left up the Via dei Crociferi. At the end it opens into the Piazza dei Crociferi, where to the left you will see the church of:

3. **Santa Maria in Trivio.** This small church has an interesting story behind it. Legend states that it was built by the famous Roman general Belisarius in the 6th century as an act of contrition for deposing Pope Silverius and sending him into exile. The church was rebuilt in 1575 by architect Jacopo del Duca.

Turning to your right, you will probably see a huge crowd of people. Walk up this street (Via Poli) and you will find yourself at the:

4. **Fontana di Trevi.** This is perhaps the most consistently mobbed tourist site in Rome. It is also spectacularly beautiful. This enormous baroque masterpiece—it takes up the whole rear facade of the Palazzo Poli—was built in 1762 in a style inspired by the baroque master Giovanni Lorenzo Bernini. The name Trevi refers to the intersection of three roads *(tre vie)* in the nearby piazza. The theme of the fountain derives from the Aqua Virgo, an aqueduct finished at the time of Agrippa (19 B.C.); even in ancient times there was a fountain here, which marked the place where the waters entered the city. The ancient fountain was rebuilt in 1453, and the current one was begun in 1732. It isn't hard to see why it took decades to complete. It resembles nothing so much as a giant mythological stage set executed in stone, with the building of the palace as a backdrop. A huge statue of the ocean god, rising from the deep, dominates the center of the fountain. In front of him two Tritons reign in the winged horses that guide his chariot (hard to see, but in the form of a shell). The figures are cleverly made to appear to be hewn out of natural rock outcroppings.

Turning your back to the fountain, turn right into the pedestrian street Via delle Muratte, which is lined with shops, restaurants, and cafes. When you come to Via

Santa Maria in Via again, turn left. This will shortly bring you to the:

5. **Palazzo Sciarra.** This building is an open-air gallery in Art Nouveau style (like that of the Galleria Colonna). The gallery was created as part of the reconstruction of the surrounding palazzo; it was frescoed inside by Giuseppe Cellini and finished in 1886. If you turn left in front of the palazzo on Via Minghetti and walk half a block, then turn right on Via della Vergine, you will come to the entrance of the **Teatro Quirino,** one of the most important theaters in the city; it offers a richly varied program, from contemporary plays to classic Italian works such as commedia dell'arte.

Walk through the gallery to Via di San Marcello (late at night the gallery will be closed; in that case, just walk around the block of Teatro Quirino to get to the other side). Walking up Via di San Marcello brings you to the long rectangular Piazza dei Santi Apostoli, named for the:

6. **Basilica dei Santi Apostoli.** This church was built as early as 570 and was first renovated in the 14th century. The beautiful portico with its statues of Christ and the apostles dates from a later and more extensive rebuild in the 17th century. Inside the portico are some very early works, including a Roman relief carving of an eagle from the 2nd century. The inside of the church is encrusted with gilt and plasterwork in typical baroque style; among the principal artworks is the monument of Pope Clement XIV (1789), the first work to be executed in Rome by the great northern Italian sculptor Antonio Canova.

To the left of the basilica is **Palazzo dei Santi Apostoli,** designed by Giuliano da Sangallo and built in 1478–80 for a cardinal of the powerful Della Rovere family. Entering at number 51, you find two beautiful cloisters, of the late 15th and early 16th century, respectively. The latter contains the cenotaph of Michelangelo, who was briefly interred here after his death in 1564 following an illness. The story (apparently true) goes that the great artist's nephew came to Rome to collect his uncle's few remaining possessions—Michelangelo had burned many papers and drawings—and took the opportunity to carry away his body as well, hidden in a bale of hay. With great fanfare, the body of Michelangelo was buried in Florence, where it remains today.

Past the basilica and farther up the piazza is the:

7. **Palazzo Colonna,** a magnificent palace built on the site of an ancient castle of the Tuscolani family. Housed within the palace is the **Galleria Colonna** (📞 **06/6784350**), a picture gallery not to be confused with the indoor-outdoor mercantile space mentioned above. The collection in the gallery is based on the personal holdings of cardinal Girolamo Colonna acquired in the 17th century, and later expanded by other members of the family. Among the artists whose work is represented are Tintoretto, Bronzino, Carracci, and Ghirlandaio. Admission is charged. (The entrance of the Galleria Colonna is at number 66 of the Piazza dei Santi Apostoli.)

The open end of the piazza fronts on one of the busiest streets in Rome, the Via IV Novembre. Avoid it by taking the Vicolo del Piombo, just across from the Palazzo Colonna. This narrow street runs along the side of the:

8. **Palazzo Odescalchi,** another great Renaissance palace, which has passed through the hands of several prominent noble families over the centuries—the Colonna, the Chigi, and others. It was begun by Carlo Maderno, but Giovanni Lorenzo Bernini is responsible for the baroque facade (erected in 1664) facing the Piazza Santi Apostoli.

The Vicolo del Piombo will bring you out on another busy avenue, the Via del Corso. Directly across from you is the:

9. **Palazzo Doria Pamphilj,** residence of another Roman aristocratic family. Among the many remarkable things about this palace are that the family resides there to this day and that it houses one of Rome's most important private art collections. The house of cardinal Nicolò Acciapacci was built on this site in the 1400s, but it has been swept away by hundreds of years of construction and reconstruction. The current building's ornate and curiously decorated facade on the Corso is by Gabriele Valvassori and was finished in 1734. The palazzo's lavish apartments are filled with tapestries, beautiful furnishings, and art—some of which you can visit, a rare opportunity to see what it was

like to live in an aristocratic palace in all its glory. The
Galleria Doria Pamphilj (© 06/6797323) includes
works by Filippo Lippi, Raphael, Caravaggio, Tiziano,
Algardi, Vasari, Lorenzo Lotto, and others. One of the
highlights is Velázquez's portrait of Pope Innocent X,
which shares a room with a bust of the same subject by
Bernini. Admission is charged. (The entrance to the
gallery is actually around the corner in the Piazza del
Collegio Romano; see below.)

Walk along the front of Palazzo Doria Pamphilj and
turn left on Via Lata, along its right side. This will bring
you to:

10. **Piazza del Collegio Romano,** a broad square dominated by the college for which it is named. Founded at the
behest of St. Ignatius Loyola, the college occupied several
sites from 1551 to 1582, when Pope Gregory XIII initiat-
ed the construction of this imposing building. You can
still make out the pope's heraldic symbols (including the
papal tiara and keys) in a niche below the clock, which
was once used to set the time for all the clocks in the city.
The tower to the right was built much later (1787) for
meteorological and celestial observations. On the left side
of the square is the entrance to the Galleria Doria
Pamphilj (see above).

Continue walking and you will reach, on the other side
of the piazza, the:

11. **Via del Pie' di Marmo (Street of the Marble
Foot).** There really is such a foot—it came from a giant
female statue of antiquity and was placed at the end of the
street where it meets the Piazza del Collegio Romano.
However, in 1878 it was moved into the Via di Santo
Stefano del Cacco (branching off just to your left) because
it was in the way of the funeral procession for Vittorio
Emanuele II. For some reason the foot never got moved
back, but you can see it just as you turn left into the:

Via di Santo Stefano del Cacco. You can then continue down this street and look at the church for which the
street is named:

12. **Santo Stefano del Cacco** actually stands on the site of
the ancient temple to Isis and Serapis (the Iseo

Campense), and it is from this temple that the church gets its name: "cacco" is short for *macaco,* or macaque, and refers to a statue, found on this site, of an Egyptian deity with the head of a monkey. (The statue is now in the Vatican Museums.) A church has stood here from a very early date; the current building was restored in the 12th century, and again in the early 17th century. The bell tower and the apse, however, are from the 12th.

Retrace your steps and turn left, continuing on Via del Pie' di Marmo. This will turn into Via Santa Caterina da Siena, which brings you around the side of:

13. **Basilica di Santa Maria sopra Minerva,** famously the only remaining Gothic church in Rome (though this version of Gothic looks very little like the familiar French version). Around 50 B.C., Pompey the Great built a temple here dedicated to Minerva, the Roman goddess of wisdom. In 752, Pope Zacharias first built the church of Santa Maria sopra Minerva (St. Mary above Minerva), but that building was later destroyed. The current church was constructed in the 13th century but has been renovated many times, including by such eminences as Sangallo and Maderno, giving it—like most of the rest of Rome—somewhat of a baroque overlay. The church is filled with great works of art, foremost of which are Michelangelo's statue of Christ risen from the tomb, the late-15th-century frescoes of Filippino Lippi, and a funeral monument carved by Bernini. Beneath the church's main altar is the tomb of Saint Catherine of Siena.

Outside the church, note toward the right of the steps the marks on the wall indicating the flood levels of the Tiber, starting from the flood of 1422. In front of the church is the:

14. **Piazza della Minerva,** which is an attraction in its own right, particularly for an object that has become one of the most familiar images of Rome. This is the little statue of an elephant with an obelisk projecting from its back. This amalgam was conceived by Giovanni Lorenzo Bernini, at the request of Pope Alexander VII, who wanted a statue that symbolized the strength of holy knowledge. The elephant was carved by Ercole Ferrata (1667);

the obelisk, on the other hand, is a genuine Egyptian work of the 6th century B.C., which was found in 1665 in the area of the Iseo Campense. The Latin inscription on the statue's base reads, in part, "Whoever sees the carved images of the wisdom of Egypt on the obelisk carried by the elephant, the strongest of animals, will realize that it is a robust mind which sustains a solid wisdom."

Exit the piazza at the northwest end, taking the Via della Minerva. The huge brick building to your left as you walk along is actually the side of the Pantheon. This street takes you into the:

15. **Piazza della Rotonda,** the square in front of the Pantheon, and one of the most charming and atmospheric spots in Rome. This piazza has been a favorite of tourists and Romans for centuries—a plaque on one building records the stay here of Torquato Tasso, the great Italian poet of *Gerusalemme Liberata,* in the 1560s. The central fountain was designed by Giacomo della Porta and carved by Leonardo Sormani in 1575 from African marble. The steps around the fountain are a popular meeting place for Romans and visitors. The addition of a McDonald's restaurant on the square has provided a palpable aroma of bubbling grease, but not even that can reduce its charm.

Take a Break   To the east of the square you will notice a yellow sign saying **Tazza d'Oro,** or "golden cup." This is truly accurate, for in this cafe you can get a wonderful cup of espresso—or better yet, the house specialty, which is *granità di caffè.* This is a sinfully delicious concoction of frozen coffee with heavy whipped cream; as a pick-me-up, this combination of caffeine and sugar is just right.

The center of the piazza is, of course, the:

16. **Pantheon,** considered by many to be the most perfect work of architecture ever. Before creating his dome for St. Peter's, Michelangelo studied the Pantheon to see how it was done (the Pantheon's dome is actually slightly larger than that of St. Peter's). The building was first erected by the emperor Augustus's friend Marcus Vipsanius Agrippa

in 27 B.C. (the Latin inscription at the top of the portico reads "Marcus Agrippa, son of Lucius, consul for the third time, built this"), but was later destroyed. The current building was designed by the emperor Hadrian and completed in A.D. 126. The building has been modified several times since: Constantine II removed the bronze roof in 663; bell towers were added in the 1600s (Romans called them "asses ears") and removed in the 1880s. The most famous abuse of the building was by Pope Urban VIII, who took bronze cladding from the Pantheon's porch and melted it down for Bernini's baldachin in St. Peter's and for cannon in Castel Sant'Angelo. And yet, what remains is truly magnificent. Sixteen granite columns support the front of the building, each over 15m high (50 ft.) and made of a single piece of stone. The enormous bronze doors—each weighing 20 tons—open onto the perfectly round temple where sacrifices were once performed. The interior is dressed in multicolored marble and porphyry, and the round hole in the ceiling through which you can see the blue sky of Rome is sublime. Raphael's tomb is inside the Pantheon, as is that of Vittorio Emanuele II.

Facing the Pantheon, turn right and walk up the Salita dei Crescenzi; take your first left, which will shortly bring you to:

17. **Piazza Sant'Eustachio,** named for the church of St. Eustachio that faces the piazza. The story goes that the church, founded by the emperor Constantine, rests on the spot where Eustachio was martyred. Note the carving of a deer with a cross between his horns on the facade, which refers to a vision that the saint had in the forest. The church was rebuilt in 1196 (the bell tower dates from this time), and again in the 18th century.

Continue around in front of the church, bearing right. Turning into Via della Dogana Vecchia, you pass behind:

18. **Palazzo della Sapienza,** the site of the first University of Rome, founded by Pope Boniface VIII in 1303. The current building (which houses Rome's archives) was constructed in the 16th and early 17th centuries and was a work of many hands, including Giacomo della Porta and Francesco Borromini. The interior has a graceful courtyard

lined with two orders of columns; Borromini also added the church of **St. Ivo** toward the back of the courtyard; its elegant and almost whimsical spiral cupola is unique. Inside is a painting by Pietro da Cortona. (You can walk around to the entrance on Corso del Rinascimento if you wish to visit; then retrace your steps and continue the itinerary.)

Continuing up Via della Dogana Vecchia, you pass behind the:

19. **Palazzo Madama,** which has been the meeting place of the Italian senate since shortly after unification in 1871. The palace dates from 1503 and was built for a member of the Medici family.

Continuing along Via della Dogana Vecchia, you come to the church of:

20. **San Luigi dei Francesi,** the French national church in Rome (statues of Charlemagne and Saint Louis decorate the facade). It was designed by Giacomo della Porta and finished in 1589. The interior is a masterpiece of gilt, plaster, and marble work, and contains important paintings by Guido Reni, Domenichino, and others. What most tourists come to see, however, are three astounding paintings of scenes from the life of St. Matthew by Caravaggio, executed between 1599 and 1602. Their glorious color, innovative use of light, and dynamic composition are breathtaking.

Just after San Luigi dei Francesi on the opposite side of the street is the opening of the Largo Toniolo; turn right here, and continue on the Via delle Cornacchie, a narrow street that takes you past small shops and restaurants in one of the most atmospheric parts of the neighborhood. On your left, you will come to:

21. **Santa Maria Maddalena,** a church that underwent various phases of construction during the 17th century but whose facade dates from 1735. Richly decorated with stucco, statues, and other details (one might almost say frills), it is a fine example of the rococo style.

Continue along (the street name changes to Via delle Colonnelle) with the church to your left. This will bring you out in front of the:

22. **Palazzo Capranica,** an early Renaissance palace dating from 1451. It has undergone many revisions, and in 1922 was turned into the Cinema Capranica, one of the oldest movie theaters still operating in Rome.

   To your right is a narrow alley called the:

23. **Vicolo della Spada d'Orlando,** which takes its name from a marble column in the wall on the left-hand side of the alley. Popular legend has it that the chip taken out of the column was done by the sword of the knight Orlando. In reality, the column was part of a temple that the emperor Hadrian had built to commemorate the death of his mother-in-law in A.D. 119.

   Follow the alley to the end and turn left on Via de' Pastini, which brings you into:

24. **Piazza di Pietra.** The emperor Antoninus Pius had an imposing temple built here in 145, honoring Hadrian (who, in a tradition that had become established by that time, was deified after his death). In one of the most interesting examples of Roman reuse of ancient ruins, the remains of the temple were incorporated into a new building in 1695, which today houses the Roman stock exchange. You can see 11 original columns of the temple along one side, as well as much smaller bits and pieces.

   Cross the piazza and take the Via Bergamaschi to your left. This leads into:

25. **Piazza Colonna,** in the center of which is the column carved with reliefs representing the victories of Marcus Aurelius in his German and Sarmatian campaigns (A.D. 172–75) The top of the column was originally graced by a statue of the philosopher-emperor, which disappeared sometime in the Middle Ages. In the late 16th century, Pope Sixtus V had the bronze statue of St. Paul placed at the top of the column, which you see today. There was also originally a temple to Marcus Aurelius in the area of the piazza. The building that you see opposite you on the other side of the column is the **Palazzo Chigi,** which is now the main seat of the executive branch of the Italian government (it houses the Consiglio dei Ministri, or council of ministers). The palace was begun by the Aldobrandini family in 1580, who built the central

section. It later passed to the Chigi, and the wings on the sides were added. The buildings on the east side of the piazza were demolished at the end of the 19th century when the Via del Corso was enlarged.

From the Piazza Colonna, you can see another square opening off to the left of the Palazzo Chigi. This is the:

26. **Piazza di Montecitorio,** another very important political center for the state of Italy. The massive **Palazzo Montecitorio,** where the Italian parliament now meets, was begun by Pope Innocent X in 1653 following a design by (who else) Giovanni Lorenzo Bernini. Construction went on for decades and was taken over by Carlo Fontana in 1694. The red granite obelisk in the center of the piazza was brought back from Egypt during the time of Augustus and dates from about 590 B.C. The obelisk is actually a sundial; the shadow it casts indicates the hour by markings set in the pavement. The obelisk fell down in the 9th century but was restored by Pope Pio VI in 1792.

Return to the Palazzo Colonna. From here, you can cross the busy Corso and walk up a few steps to your starting point, Piazza San Silvestro, which opens to your left.

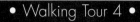
Piazza di Spagna

Start: Metro stop Flaminio.

Finish: Metro stop Flaminio.

Time: 2½ hours, excluding time for visits.

Best Time: Late afternoon Monday through Saturday; time it so you'll be on the terrace of the Pincio (at the end of our itinerary) by sunset.

Worst Time: Sundays and the lunch lull when churches are closed to visits.

W ell known to visitors around the world and many modern Romans only as the city's upscale shopping mecca, the neighborhood of Piazza di Spagna hides an interesting history and many lesser-known monuments, tucked away behind the glamorous facade of designer boutiques, jewelry stores, and museum-quality antiques shops.

This neighborhood was born during the Renaissance in an area that had been sparsely used in Roman times and then completely abandoned in the Middle Ages when Rome had shrunk back to the riverbanks. While portions of the Campus Martius that lay closer to the Roman Forum (see Walking Tour 1) had been developed under Rome's various emperors, this

Piazza di Spagna

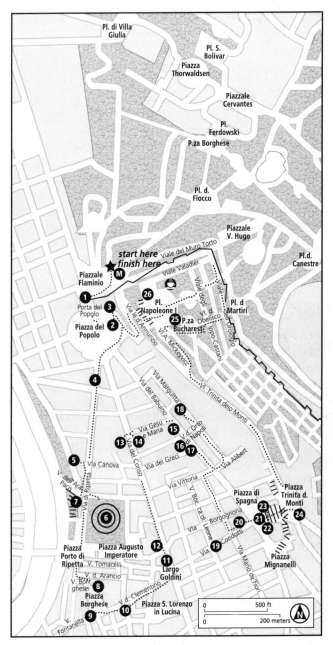

Pl. di Villa Giulia

Pl. S. Bolivar

Piazza Thorwaldsen

Piazzale Cervantes

Pl. Ferdowski

P.za Borghese

Pl. d. Fiocco

Piazzale V. Hugo

Pl.d. Canestre

start here
finish here

Viale del Muro Torto

M

Piazzale Flaminio

Viale Valadier

① ②

Porta del Popolo

③

Piazza del Popolo

26

Pl. Napoleone I

25

P.za Bucharest

Pl. d Martiri

V. d. Obelisco

Viale degi

Via degl Orologio

Vi. dippo-Castani

Via d'Annunzio

Via A. McKevic2

④

Via Marguitta

Vl. Trinita deio Monti

Via dei Babuino

18

Via Gesù e Maria

15

V. d. Orto di Napoli

13 14

16 17

Via dei Greci

Via Alibert

⑤

Via Canova

V. dell'Ara Pacis

Via di Ripetta

Via Vittoria

V. Bot. ra di Leone

Via di Borgognona

Piazza di Spagna

Piazza Trinita d. Monti

23

⑦

6

20

21 24

22

Via Condotti

Via Mario de Fiori

19

Piazza Mignanelli

12

Piazza Porto di Ripetta

Piazza Augusto Imperatore

V. Tomacelli

11

Largo Goldini

V. d. Arancio

8

V. Bot. ghesei

Piazza Borghese

V. d. Clementino

10

Piazza S. Lorenzo in Lucina

9

V. Fontanella

| 0 | 500 ft |
| 0 | 200 meters |

N

further section remained rather uninhabited in Roman times, even though it existed within the city's Aurelian Wall. For centuries the area remained lightly urbanized; it held little more than a hospital and a few settlements of pilgrims from Dalmatia and Illiria centered around the commercial wharves on the Tiber near the Mausoleum of Augustus (see stop 6, below).

All this changed in 1512 with Pope Leo X and his *Tridente* ("trident"), an urbanization plan that had three main prongs: the existing Via Flaminia (the ancient Roman road that runs from the Capitoline Hill in the direction of Tuscany, passing the walls under today's Porta del Popolo) and two new streets, Via del Babuino and Via di Ripetta. The three main arteries were then connected with transversal streets; of these, the most important was the Via Trinitatis, which closed the trident to the south and ran from the river to Piazza di Spagna. This street was laid out in 1544 and today comprises the Via del Clementino, Via di Fontanella Borghese, and Via dei Condotti).

Elegant buildings sprang up to line the newly created streets, beginning with the Palazzo Borghese (see stop 8, below) at the end of 16th century. By the 18th century, additional development took place with the construction of a proper harbor near the Augustus Mausoleum (the Porto di Ripetta, built in 1703–04 and destroyed 200 years later by the new embankments on the Tiber). The grand Scalinata di Trinità dei Monti—the famous Spanish Steps (see stop 21)— were also built in this period. The final touch was the scenic arrangement of Piazza del Popolo with the construction in 1834 of the Passeggiata del Pincio (promenade of the Pincio).

Unfortunately, perfection rarely endures for long. This splendid baroque neighborhood had to suffer first from the marginal demolitions along the Tiber that made way for construction of new river embankments and the Lungotevere. The neighborhood suffered again (and more substantially) between 1937 and 1940, when a large section of the tight urban fabric was destroyed to "isolate" the Mausoleum of Augustus. This approach was inaugurated by the Fascist regime—which had great admiration for the Roman Empire. The Fascists' urban planners endeavored to visually highlight the remaining great monuments from the ancient Roman era by destroying surrounding buildings—medieval, Renaissance, or whatever—that "obscured" them (see Walking Tour 1, for example). Sadly, they were successful in their endeavors. No doubt it made for better postcards, but much that was irreplaceable was lost. Luckily, this slash-and-burn approach did not prevail for long, and today the neighborhood is dense with wonderful buildings and a stimulating atmosphere.

• • • • • • • • • • • • • • • •

Exit from the Metro station Flaminio and proceed straight across Via del Muro Torto (make sure to cross at the light, as this is a busy road) to the city walls. Pass under the:

1. **Porta del Popolo (Gate of the People).** This elaborate entrance into Piazza del Popolo dates from the baroque period. Giovanni Lorenzo Bernini altered the original design of this city gate in 1655, adding the heraldic symbols of Pope Alexander VII and of Queen Christine of Sweden—who Romans greeted with enthusiasm following her abdication from the throne. A brilliant and fearless woman, she was raised a Lutheran but gradually turned toward Catholicism and brought her brilliant circle of friends with her when she moved to Rome. Her symbol—flowers of wheat—has left a permanent mark on the Porta del Popolo. Among other changes, the two 15th-century towers that flanked the portal were demolished in the late 19th century to add the two smaller arches to either side of the gate.

   Once through the portal, you'll find yourself in:

2. **Piazza del Popolo,** one of Rome's most scenic squares. It was renovated in the 17th century and given its present aspect by the architect Giuseppe Valadier in 1816. The branching point of the *Tridente* (the trident of streets ordered by Pope Leo X) is composed of the Via del Babuino to the left, Via del Corso to the middle, and Via di Ripetta to the right (see below). This square was meant to be the monumental entrance to Rome and was embellished by several popes through the baroque period. The central fountain dates from 1572 and the obelisk—the oldest in Rome, a granite Egyptian monolith dating from 1200 B.C.—was added a few years later in 1589 when it was brought here from its original place in the Circus

Maximus. The twin churches on either side of the Corso were added in the 17th century. In the early 19th century, Valadier redesigned the central fountain and added the fountains to either side. Valadier constructed the buildings at the head of each of the two lateral streets of the trident. He also created the scenic promenade up the Pincio to the east of the square, resulting in the city's first public park (see Giardini del Pincio later). Already in the baroque period, Piazza del Popolo had acquired an important social role in Rome as the site of fairs and celebrations—and also of capital executions—which it maintained in later centuries. It became one of the "salons" of the city in the 19th century, when two elegant cafes (still extant today), Caffè Canova at the corner of Via del Babuino and Caffè Rosati at the corner of Via di Ripetta, became favorite hangouts for the cream of Roman society.

On the square, immediately to your left after you pass through the gate, is the church of:

3. **Santa Maria del Popolo.** This church is renowned for the two splendid paintings by Caravaggio in the left transept (the conversion of St. Paul and the crucifixion of St. Peter), as well as the frescoes by Pinturicchio in the choir. But few people are aware of the curious history of the church itself, which was created from the enlargement and modification of a preexisting chapel, which in turn was constructed in the year 1099 over the Domitian's mausoleum where the notorious emperor Nero is buried. The chapel was built using money from the people of Rome, hence its name, which translates as "St. Mary of the People." Many big names in Italian art and architecture are linked to this church, from Bramante who designed the choir, to Raphael who designed the Cappella Chigi (second to the left), to Bernini, who rearranged the facade and the interior. Other lesser-known masterpieces are the marble altar created by Andrea Bregno in 1473 in the sacristy, the two funeral monuments in the choir by Andrea Sansovino from 1507, and the monument and busts by Alessandro Algardi in the third chapel to the left.

Cross the square, admiring the perspective created by the promenade to the Giardini del Pincio (see later) at your left, and take the furthest right of the three long, straight streets of the "trident" departing from the square. This is:

4. **Via di Ripetta.** Built in 1517–19 over a preexisting ancient Roman street, this was named Via Leonina in honor of Pope Leo X who planned its reconstruction. In the 18th century the street was renamed Porto di Ripetta because it led to the new *porto* (harbor) near the Mausoleum of Augustus.

   Continue along this street, passing Via Canova to your left where, at number 16, was the studio of the famous sculptor. Across is the:

5. **Accademia delle Belle Arti,** Rome's Beaux Arts Academy. Built over the dock area of what was the Ripetta harbor, where wood and goods arrived downriver from Tuscany and Umbria, this 19th-century building has been labeled "the horseshoe" from the shape of the central body connecting the two lateral wings.

   From the atrium of the academy you can reach the Passeggiata di Ripetta, a shaded promenade along the Tiber designed by Giuseppe Valadier in the 19th century. Here you will also find the Liberty (Art Nouveau) boathouse of the Circolo Canottieri Aniene, a long-established rowing club.

   Retrace your steps to Via di Ripetta and continue on to Piazza Augusto Imperatore, dominated by the:

6. **Mausoleo di Augusto (Mausoleum of Augustus).** Much more modest than the mausoleum built by Emperor Hadrian, the Mausoleum of Augustus reflects an earlier time that reflects the more restrained spirit of the Roman republic. The wide open space around the mausoleum was created during the Fascist period by pulling down the buildings that had grown up over the years, essentially destroying an entire neighborhood. Augustus began the monument for himself and his family in 27 B.C., but like other buildings in Rome it went through many other incarnations—vineyard, garden, amphitheater, and auditorium. Originally, the monument was topped by a pillar and a statue of Augustus.

   Turn right from the square and cross Via di Ripetta, which separates the mausoleum from the:

7. **Ara Pacis Augustae (Altar of Augustan Peace).**
The altar was commissioned by Augustus, Rome's first
emperor, and finished in 9 B.C. The Ara Pacis is a monument that celebrated Roman "pacification" (used in its
modern sense of the bringing of peace through war) of
Gaul and Spain. It was discovered in the 16th century on
Piazza San Lorenzo in Lucina, near what is now the Via
del Corso (which was in Roman times the Via Flaminia,
a road that led north out of Rome, and hence to Gaul and
Spain, making this an appropriate location for the monument). The altar was moved here in 1937–38 when the
entire neighborhood was changed into its modern form.
The marble wall behind which the altar stood is over 12m
long (40 ft.) and completely covered with carvings. The
front wall illustrates the *Lupercalia,* the traditional celebration of the founding of Rome; it also shows Aeneas, a
Trojan prince and mythical forefather of Rome, offering
sacrifices to his ancestors. The short sides of the monument show the imperial family, the goddess Peace, and the
goddess Rome.

Continue on Via di Ripetta, crossing Via Tomacelli (a
quite busy street). Just after you cross Via dell' Arancio,
on your left you will see the short side of the:

8. **Palazzo Borghese.** Added in 1612–14 after the completion of the main palace, this narrow wing with hanging gardens overlooking the Tiber was designed by
Flaminio Ponzio. It was dubbed "the keyboard" by
Romans for its multiple levels of balconies and columns
(one level was later enclosed). As you walk a little further,
you see that indeed, this large palace has a trapezoidal
shape somewhat like a grand piano; hence its nickname,
the *cembalo* (clavichord) and the nickname of its terraces.
Its longest (diagonal) side stretches away from the Via di
Ripetta along Via Borghese. This massive and elaborately
decorated building was commissioned by cardinal
Camillo Borghese, and executed by Flaminio Ponzio
between 1605 and 1614, probably on a design by
Vignola. Perhaps the most imposing palazzo in Rome, it
housed the offices for the administration of the family's
growing estate, and today remains the Borghese's private
residence.

Turn left and walk along Via Borghese, which opens into:

9. **Piazza Borghese.** This is the seat of a picturesque, permanent outdoor market of rare books and antique prints. Famous for the bargains that can be had, it specializes in antique books on art and antique prints of Rome. The local vendors—similar to Paris *bouquinistes*—are generally honest and reliable, but if you are not an expert do not try to get the steal of the century on a valuable item, for you might be the only pigeon caught.

   Continue along the facade of Palazzo Borghese and turn left in:

10. **Largo Fontanella Borghese.** From a gateway here to the left, you can have a glimpse of the palazzo's inner courtyard and garden. A majestic affair surrounded by loggias and arches decorated with ancient Roman statues, it is graced at the end by a *ninfeo* decorated with more antique statues and several baroque fountains along the walls.

    Take Via Fontanella Borghese, enjoying the scenic view of the Scalinata della Trinità dei Monti (the Spanish Steps; see stop 21) at the end. Walk past Via del Leoncino to Largo Goldoni, named after Carlo Goldoni, the great Italian dramatist of the 18th century, who lived in Palazzo Manfroni at number 47 of Via Tomacelli (the other street coming into the square to your left) in 1758 and 1759. Largo Goldoni opens onto:

11. **Via del Corso.** Crossing the Campus Martius, this street retains the north–south orientation of the street it was built over: the ancient Roman Via Flaminia, a highway that led from Porta del Popolo (then Porta Flaminia) toward Tuscany and the northern provinces. With the baroque development of the neighborhood, the Via del Corso became the heart of the city; after the opening of elegant cafes in the 18th century, it grew to be the lively center of Roman intellectual life. From the 19th century on, fashion boutiques and bookstores began to open their doors here. In 1900, the Italian royal family decided to rename it Corso Umberto I (after the king who was assassinated in that year), but they were not very lucky; the

name didn't stick and it was changed back in 1947. Called by locals simply *il Corso,* it has lost much of its glamour from the 1980s onward, when many if its historical cafes and boutiques were turned into modern fashion shops.

Turn left on Via del Corso where to your left, flanked by two elegant 17th century palaces, is the imposing facade of the church of:

12. **Santi Ambrogio e Carlo al Corso,** one of the greatest examples of Roman baroque, built between 1612 and 1684 by a number of famous artists, including Pietro da Cortona, who designed the interior decorations and the cupola. The church is splendid, and you can have a better view of it by walking around the back in Piazza Augusto Imperatore from Via del Grottino (immediately before the church to your left).

Continue on Via del Corso, and again on your left, is:

13. **San Giacomo in Augusta,** a church completed in 1600 by architect and artist Carlo Maderno, and dedicated to St. James the Apostle ("in Augusta" refers to the nearby Mausoleo di Augusto). The church is also called San Giacomo degli Incurabili (St. James of the Incurables) because it is annexed to **Ospedale di San Giacomo,** a hospital founded in the 14th century that specialized in incurable diseases. The church's elegant and spacious interior is unfortunately somewhat worse for the restorations performed in the 19th century. Little remains of the hospital's original structure, which was extensively rebuilt in the 19th century.

Across the Via del Corso from San Giacomo is the church of:

14. **Gesu e Maria,** built between 1672 and 1675. The rich interior of this baroque church was financed by a local wealthy man, Giorgio Bolognetti, who was then allowed to be buried here with other members of his family. The monuments to their memory line the church's nave from above the confessionals, as though from theater balconies—a rather unique effect.

Turn right on Via Gesu e Maria and right again on:

15. **Via del Babuino.** Laid out in 1525 and completed in 1543, this street was officially named Via Paolina Trifaria, but locals always referred to it as Via del Babuino ("baboon street") from the statue of a satyr that was found and left there (see below). This street is famous for the many antiquarian shops that line it—some are a century old and among the most reputable in Rome.

    Pass, immediately to your right, the **Church of All Saints**—an English Evangelical church built in the 19th century in Gothic Revival style—and continue to the church of:

16. **Sant'Atanasio.** You can visit the unusual interior of this church, which was built in the 16th century by Giacomo della Porta and dedicated to the Greek Catholic rite. Inside are two noteworthy paintings by Cavalier d'Arpino: a Crucifixion in the left apse, and an Assumption of Mary in the right apse.

    Just past the church is the:

17. **Fontana del Babuino (Fountain of the Baboon).** Moved here in 1957, this fountain was built in 1738 using the statue of the satyr that gave its name to the street. The statue represents Sileno, a wise old satyr known to have counseled king Midas and to have educated the god Bacchus; he was also very ugly—as ugly as a baboon—according to popular wisdom. Sileno is one of the six "talking statues" of Rome, known as the *congresso degli arguti* (the council of the witty ones), who criticized the government in a lively dialogue of short and clever verses that were affixed to them during the night (see Pasquino in Walking Tour 2).

    Continue on and turn left on Via Alibert, and immediately left again on:

18. **Via Margutta.** This celebrated street is one of the most picturesque in Rome and has been lined with artist studios—you can see the large windows looking north—since the 17th century. Each year it livens up with the **Cento Pittori Via Margutta** fair, when a hundred selected painters exhibit their work right on the street, turning it into a huge open-air gallery. The event takes place in November and again in April/May.

Retrace your steps and cross Via del Babuino into Via Vittoria—probably named after the sister of King Louis XVI who took refuge in the monastery here to escape the aftermath of the French Revolution. The convent today is the seat of the Accademia Nazionale di Santa Cecilia, one of the most famous music conservatories in the world.

Turn left on Via Mario de' Fiori ("Mario of the Flowers"), named after the 17th-century painter Mario Nuzzi, who specialized in floral still-lifes. Today it is lined with famous boutiques. Turn left again on:

19. **Via dei Condotti,** one of the most famous places in Rome for elegant shopping—together with the nearby Via Belsiana, Via Bocca di Leone, Via Frattina, and Via Borgognona. While many visitors in Rome know that they'll find here some of the best names in the fashion industry, few ever look above the windows of the boutiques that line this street. If you do, you will see a line of elegant *palazzi* that made the street famous back in the 17th and 18th centuries. Even fewer know the origin of this street's name ("street of the conduits," or pipelines), which derives from the three conduits that passed here and brought the water of the Acqua Vergine aqueduct to the Trevi fountain (see Walking Tour 3). Just as cities sometimes have partners or "twins" in other countries, the Via dei Condotti is, appropriately enough, twinned with Bond Street in London.

Immediately to your left, at number 86, is the famous:

20. **Caffè Greco.** The cafe was opened by a Greek—Nicola di Maddalena, as it says on the plaque outside—in 1760, and it rapidly became the headquarters of the city's literary and artistic leaders and a focus of cultural life. It is also Rome's oldest cafe—it has remained in operation since its opening—and is decorated inside with its original furnishings. It feels a bit like a private gallery, with paintings by its talented patrons (such as Corot). Among the famous patrons are also writers—Goldoni, Leopardi, D'Annunzio, Gogol, Byron, Henry James, Stendhal—and musicians, such as Wagner and Mendelssohn, and even Buffalo Bill (yes, William Frederick Cody), who left his signed photograph in 1906. Run by a group since the

Gubinelli family—which had run the cafe since 1873—left in 1999, it continues to offer excellent service and unique atmosphere.

Via dei Condotti offers a perfect scenic approach to:

21. **Piazza di Spagna and the Spanish Steps.** Originally named Piazza Trinitatis for the church at the top of the steps, it became "di Spagna" (of Spain) in honor of the palace of the Spanish Ambassador there. It was the cultural and tourist heart of Rome from the start, with hotels and inns lining its sides. Most of the original buildings are still there, although with additional floors built in the 19th century (in the 17th c. most buildings were only two stories high). The fountain—locally know as the *barcaccia* (the ugly boat)—was created by the Berninis, father Giovanni and son Pietro, in 1629 and cleverly built slightly lower than street level to solve the problem of water pressure. The proper name of the Spanish Steps is Scalinata della Trinità dei Monti; they were built between 1723 and 1726, replacing the steep wooded trails that climbed up the slope of the Pincio to finally provide the church above them with proper access. The fountain and the steps are a favorite meeting spot for the young—and noisy—crowds of both Romans and tourists. In the late afternoons of spring and summer it is almost impossible to walk up the steps.

    Framing the steps on each side are two 18th-century buildings; to your right at number 26 is the:

22. **Casina Rossa (Little Red House),** is also called the Keats-Shelley House. This was the poet John Keats's home when he died in 1821. A year later his good friend and fellow poet Percy Bysshe Shelley drowned. The house was transformed into a museum at the beginning of the 20th century; it includes many of Keats's personal mementos, as well as his eerie death mask. The Keats-Shelley Memorial foundation houses a library and a permanent exhibit on the two poets and writers.

    Opposite at number 22 is:

23. **Babington's,** Rome's first—and for a long time only—tearoom. British aficionados can sip their brew in perfect English style in this original tearoom (actually tea

"rooms," as it specifies on the sign), which opened in 1893. Babington is trying to promote its brand name, offering possibilities of franchising and a shop with elegant packaged products with its logo; this, together with its steep prices and less-than-perfect quality of both brews and food, make it into your classic tourist trap, but it's still worth peeking inside.

Climb the famous steps up to:

24. **Piazza della Trinità dei Monti,** opening as a terrace over the city. The obelisk here originally belonged to the villa of Sallust that existed nearby; its hieroglyphs are Roman copies from a real Egyptian obelisk. The church giving its name to this *piazza* and to the steps is a French Catholic church built in the 16th century by King Louis XII. The interior and attached convent are richly decorated with frescoes, but only the first half of the church is usually open to the public, the remainder being fenced off by a gate.

Turn left on Viale Trinità dei Monti, past **Villa Medici,** the beautiful 16th-century palace that houses the French Art Academy and its library. Up here you are on the Pincio, a hill that in Roman times was the location of several elegant villas belonging to important patricians. The most beautiful was the *Horti Lucullani,* the villa of a man named Lucullus famous for his lavish banquets. Some of its rooms and walls are still visible in the basement of both Villa Medici and the Convent of the Sacred Heart, attached to the church of the Trinità dei Monti. Continue up on Viale Mickiewicz, keeping to your right.

Turn right into Viale dell'Obelisco, entering the:

25. **Giardini del Pincio.** The plans for these gardens were made by the French architect Berthault for Napoleon during his brief rule of the city. He wanted to create a Promenade Publique for the enjoyment of all citizens in the typical French style. The suggested name for the gardens was Jardin du Grand César. But Napoleon fell from power and never moved the capital of his empire to Rome; however, the project remained and Pope Pius VII called in the architect Giuseppe Valadier to translate it into reality. The gardens are divided from Villa Borghese

(see Walking Tour 10) by the curving wall that gives its name to the Viale del Muro Torto (literally, "Alley of the Winding Wall") below. Segments of this wall incorporate the Aurelian city walls from the 4th century A.D., and part is the embankment created to support the terraced gardens of an ancient Roman Villa.

Viale dell'Obelisco—lined with busts of famous Italians—ends in the viaduct over the Via del Muro Torto, created in 1908, which connects the Pincio with Villa Borghese. Turn left on Viale dell'Orologio to admire the **water clock** built in 1867, and left again onto the main alley leading to:

26. **Piazzale Napoleone I,** with a terrace overlooking Piazza del Popolo and Rome's most famous panorama. Very popular with young (and also middle-aged and older) couples but also with anybody loving a good sunset, it becomes crowded on fair days, when the light tints the walls and domes of the Eternal City with glorious gold.

Take a Break You can have an *aperitivo,* dinner, or just an espresso at the **Casina Valadier,** the stylish cafe—with restaurant, wine bar, and panoramic terrace—which has been revived after a 2-year-long restoration. The cafe, closed for decades, was created by the architect Giuseppe Valadier in 1817, transforming the preexisting *Casino della Rota,* a 16th-century "lodge" built over an ancient Roman cistern. The creative menu offers simpler choices at lunch and more elaborate fare in the evening, but the "in" thing is definitely the *aperitivo,* especially at sunset (and provided you can get in).

Descend the steps down the **Passeggiata del Pincio,** which were also created by Valadier as a scenic promenade and are decorated with fountains and groups of statues. This will bring you from the Pincio gardens down to Piazza del Popolo. From the piazza, you can walk back to the Metro stop Flaminio where you started.

Campo de' Fiori

Start: Largo di Torre Argentina (tram 8; bus 62, 64, 87, 119, or 492).

Finish: Largo di Torre Argentina.

Time: 2½ hours.

Best Time: Mornings after rush hour, when the Campo's market is still open, or 3pm to dusk.

Worst Time: During rush hours, when traffic and noise are worst.

Campo de' Fiori is one of those places in Rome where the layers of the past, to use geological terminology, are most compressed and folded together, creating a sort of metamorphic whole: A vegetable seller now hawks his produce on the spot where Giordano Bruno was immolated, and laundry hangs from windows in buildings rising atop the ruins of an ancient Roman theater. You can line up with the locals for some of the best focaccia in town while gazing upon the architectural perfection of one of the most imposing palaces in the city, built for the Farnese, one of the city's most illustrious families. In fact, this is one of the few areas of the city that was never abandoned, not even during the Dark Ages; Romans of one kind or another have been living here continuously for more than 2,000 years.

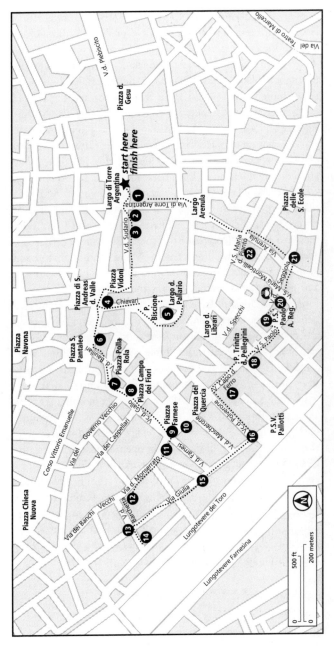

The neighborhood of Campo de' Fiori used to be seamlessly connected to that of Piazza Navona (see Walking Tour 2), but one of the postunification urban projects was the construction of Corso Vittorio Emanuele II, which was rammed through medieval and Renaissance neighborhoods, with, as usual, more respect for the latter than the former (the 19th c. idealized the Renaissance, but often denigrated the Middle Ages). However, a warren of medieval streets punctuated with grand Renaissance palaces still surrounds the Campo. The itinerary below leads you to many beautiful sights, but there is one attraction that has no address: the atmosphere. It's everywhere.

Bordering the river Tiber, this neighborhood was marshy—even with some volcanic springs—during ancient times. It was first developed in the 2nd century B.C., and included arsenals (convenient to the nearby Campus Martius) and surrounding dwellings. Later it would see the construction of important civic buildings such as the stadium of Domitian and the theater of Pompey. After the collapse of the Roman Empire and the shrinkage of the city to a mere town, the area benefited from the rise of the Vatican: The Campo de' Fiori sat astride the "Via Peregrinorum," the route that pilgrims took to visit St. Peter's Basilica. Some ancient buildings were "englobed"—turned to new uses and incorporated into new structures, sometimes to the point of being unrecognizable—while others disappeared. A dense collection of buildings grew along this important route, to the point that, at the beginning of the Renaissance, it was one of the few areas of the city where there were more buildings than open spaces (though the Campo itself was grassy—hence the name de' Fiori, "of flowers"). Long before Italian unification, the neighborhood became the target of urban "renewal," beginning with the Jubilee year of 1425. Later popes continued the process (demolitions for new streets were also undertaken by the Fascist regime in the 20th century), which has yielded the combination of straight streets and crooked alleys that we see today.

●　●　●　●　●　●　●　●　●　●　●　●　●　●　●

Exit from your bus or tram in Largo di Torre Argentina, a major transport hub. In the middle of this roughly rectangular square you will see an enormous hole with columns and trees rising out of it. This is, in fact, the:

1. **Area Sacra dell'Argentina,** which is actually the largest collection of structures dating from Rome's republican period in the city. It includes, among other things, the remains of four temples, the oldest of which is dedicated to the Italic goddess Feronia and was constructed at the beginning of the 3rd century B.C. The most preserved remains are of a temple from the middle of that century, which was later converted to a church. Interestingly, one structure of large tufa blocks has been identified with the Curia of Pompey, the place where Julius Caesar was stabbed to death in 44 B.C. You can walk around the fenced perimeter of the area and see most of the remains, but the site is not open to the public.

   Turn toward the western side of the square. Toward the corner of Corso Vittorio Emanuele II you will see the:

2. **Teatro Argentina.** This neoclassical theater is one of the leading theatrical venues in the city and has an illustrious history. In 1816, it saw the premiere of Rossini's *Barber of Seville.* The theater was built in 1732, has undergone several changes and restorations, and today is the seat of the Teatro di Roma, which is devoted to Italian drama (not opera; © **06/684000345;** www.teatrodiroma.net).

   Between the theater and the Corso Vittorio Emanuele II is a small street, the Via del Sudario. Walk up this street to number 44, which is the:

3. **Casa del Burcardo.** This house was built in 1503 by Giovanni Burckhardt, who was a native of Strasbourg, the ancient name of which was Argentoratum. This is the source of the name of the nearby tower, the Torre Argentina, for which the square is called. The house still shows the influence of German architecture of the period. Today it houses a library and collection related to theater.

   Turn right at the end of Via del Sudario into the Piazza Vidoni. Straight ahead is the Corso Vittorio Emanuele II, the major street that was begun in 1883 in order to connect to the new Via Nazionale and provide an east–west route across the burgeoning capital. Turn left on Corso Vittorio Emanuele II, and you will find yourself in the:

4. **Piazza di Sant'Andrea della Valle,** which feels less like a piazza than simply a wide spot in the Corso

Vittorio. In the center of the piazza is a fountain by Carlo Maderno (1614), the architect who took over the construction of the church you are standing in front of, **Sant'Andrea della Valle.** Maderno also designed the cupola of the church, which is actually the second tallest in Rome, after St. Peter's. Urban renewal has not been kind to this church, which sits on one of the busiest—and hardest to cross—intersections in Rome, full of cacophonous traffic. It is well worth visiting, however; with multicolored marble, stucco, and gold, it is one of the most outstanding baroque interiors of Rome. Of particular interest are the presbytery and the apse, which contain work by the sculptor Alessandro Algardi and frescoes by Domenichino.

Walk away from the Corso along the right-hand side of the church; this is the Largo dei Chiavari. At the end, continue on the Via dei Chiavari. Soon you will see to your right an arc of buildings, which are actually built atop the:

5. **Teatro di Pompeo.** Originally, Roman theaters were constructed of wood and therefore often destroyed by fire. This was the first stone theater and was constructed in 55 B.C. by Pompey (not far as the crow flies from Pompey's curia, mentioned above). Even so, it was damaged by fire in A.D. 80 and restored by the emperor Domitian. If you use your imagination, you can visualize this street of picturesque buildings as part of a theater that once held 18,000 spectators.

Retrace your steps to the Corso Vittorio Emanuele II. Walking up on the left-hand side of Corso Vittorio, you pass at number 154 the **Palazzo di Girolamo Pichi,** a once-beautiful building that was largely ruined by the opening of the Corso. Then, at number 168, you will come upon the:

6. **Farnesina ai Baullari,** which remains a wonderful example of 15th-century architecture despite having also been roughly treated during the period of urban renovation. The original design of the building is a matter of debate. It was once thought—wrongly, it turns out—to be the work of Raphael. This great artist actually died 2

years before the building was begun, in 1522, for the
Breton priest Thomas Le Roy. You might take a moment
to walk all around the building; the original facade was on
the Vicolo dell' Aquila, and is a great example of the
Renaissance sense of harmony and proportion. The opening of the Corso in the 19th century required the creation
of a new facade facing the new street, thus, the charming
loggia on the "front" of the building is an addition (by
Enrico Guj, in 1898–1904). The Farnesina ai Baullari
contains an interesting small museum, the **Museo
Barracco** (② **06/68806848**), which has a collection
designed to illustrate the history of sculpture, from
ancient Egypt and Assyria to Greece and Rome, and
includes Phoenician, Sardinian, and Etruscan works. It is
open Tuesday through Saturday from 9am to 7pm and
Sundays from 9am to 1pm. Admission is charged.

On the right (or west) side of the Farnesina ai Baullari
opens the:

7. **Piazza della Cancelleria,** the west side of which is
taken up by the **Palazzo della Cancelleria.** Most pass by
the Cancelleria, a large and striking building that is rarely
on tourist itineraries or guides. The site was originally
occupied by the **Basilica di San Lorenzo in Damaso,**
which was begun under Pope Damaso as early as A.D. 380,
and by a small palace annexed to the basilica, which
included the office of the papal archives. When, in 1483,
the basilica passed to the care of Cardinal Raffaele Riario,
he decided to transform the annexed little palace into his
residence. Work started in 1485 and was not finished
until 1513. The palace was totally reconstructed, and the
result was so strikingly beautiful that the pope decided to
confiscate the building and turn it into the papal archives.
Of the whole palace, the Cardinal Riario was allowed to
keep just an apartment, reserved as the residence for the
cardinal in charge of the basilica.

The High Renaissance style of the Cancelleria presents
an imposing, monolithic block with huge planes of travertine marble, relieved and lightened by cornices that break
the whole into three distinct levels, and the *bugnato* technique, whereby the use of small decorative blocks gives
the expanse a subtlety varied texture. You can take a peek

into the inner courtyard and admire its three orders of columns (concerts, open to the public are occasionally held in the building; look for posters in the alcove). Inscriptions on the Cancelleria attest to the varied uses it has served in the past, including as the seat of parliament during the short-lived Roman Republic, which was proclaimed here on February 9, 1848. Today the building houses offices related to the management of the papacy's vast archaeological and artistic holdings.

Walk up along the Cancelleria away from the Corso Vittorio Emanuele II, noting on the south side a **balcony** carved by Andrea Bregno. Passing on your right the Via Pellegrino, a piece of the ancient Via Peregrinorum, you find yourself in the:

8. **Campo de' Fiori.** If you arrive during a weekday morning, the sight that will greet your eyes is wall-to-wall merchants selling a vast variety of goods from vegetables to kitchen utensils to, well, junk. It is a festival of colors, sounds, and activity. Dominating the square is the somber, hooded figure of **Giordano Bruno,** burned on this spot in 1600. The bronze by Ettore Ferrari shows the philosopher holding a book containing his theories (which included that the earth revolved around the sun), for which he was condemned as a heretic. Reliefs around the base of the sculpture show scenes from his life and trial. The Campo's history goes back much farther than this; it occupies roughly what was the forecourt of the Roman temple of Venus Vincitrix, which was connected to the nearby theater of Pompey (see above).

The Campo is a place dear to the hearts of Romans, and expresses the long-suffering and irrepressible spirit of the people. The rectangular square is ringed with restaurants, cafes, pubs, bookstores, and even a movie theater. It is active morning, noon, and especially night, when it attracts a young and sometimes boisterous crowd. More shops, restaurants, and some hotels spread out in all directions along the streets leading into it.

Cross the short western side of the rectangular piazza, heading toward the tantalizing massive palazzo you see in the distance. Walking down the Vicolo del Gallo brings you into the:

9. **Piazza Farnese,** one of the most magnificent squares in Rome, but one rarely crammed with tourists (probably because there is almost nowhere to sit). The open space is punctuated with two identical fountains, thought to be the work of Girolamo Rainaldi. Their bases are made from two enormous basins of Egyptian granite that came from the **Baths of Caracalla** (see Walking Tour 9).

   To your right are two 18th-century structures, the small church of **Santa Brigida,** and at number 44 the **Palazzo del Gallo di Roccagiovine.** But dominating the square is the:

10. **Palazzo Farnese,** the most beautiful palace in Rome. Despite being the work of many hands, the word that best describes it is "perfect": Its harmony and proportion, not to mention its massiveness, are the ultimate development of Renaissance architecture in Rome. It took more than half a century to build; it was begun in 1517 at the behest of Cardinal Alessandro Farnese, who would later become Pope Paul III. This phase was conducted by the great Antonio da Sangallo il Giovane; after his death it was taken up by Michelangelo at midcentury, and finally finished by Vignola and Giacomo della Porta (in 1589). Semicircular and triangular timpani alternate in the facade, which is capped by a magnificent cornice carved with lilies (heraldic symbol of the Farnese family). For decades, the palazzo was a drab gray, the result of pollution, but a recent renovation and cleaning have left it a luminous pale yellow or cream color. You will also notice a large French tricolor hanging from the front of the palace, signifying that today it is the seat of the **French embassy** (the palace passed to the French through the Bourbon monarchy that ruled Naples). Hence the palace is now the rather grand office building of the French diplomatic service, but it can be visited by the public on selected Sundays; call the embassy at © **06/686011.** Among the wonders of the interior are the ornate stucco and marble decorations and frescoes by Domenichino. The huge **gallery** on the second floor was frescoed by Annibale Carracci with allegorical scenes and stories from classical mythology.

Standing facing the palazzo, turn right into the Via di Monserrato. On your left, you will soon see the church of:

11. **San Girolamo della Carita,** built, according to tradition, on the spot where the saint lived and died (in A.D. 382). The current church is a baroque revision with a facade by Carlo Rainaldi erected in 1660. The church contains a number of interesting works, including one of the last works of the architect Borromini, the Spada chapel (first on your right), which is decorated with marble painted to look like tapestry. In the transept to the right is a funerary monument designed by Pietro da Cortona.

On the same side of the street and just a little farther on is another church:

12. **Santa Maria in Monserrato.** The Via Monserrato derives its name from the fact that a Spanish sanctuary existed here from the early Renaissance, and indeed, Santa Maria in Monserrato is today the Spanish national church in Rome. Sangallo il Giovane began the construction in 1518, just around the time that he was beginning the Palazzo Farnese down the street (see above). Over the door of the church is a carving representing the Madonna and Child apparently sawing a mountain, which refers to a legendary Catalan monastery in Montserrat. Inside, the church is a single nave with lateral chapels; the first to the right contains a painting of *San Diego d'Alcantara* by Annibale Carracci, while the third to the left has a statue of St. James by the Florentine sculptor Jacopo Sansovino.

Further on, Via Monserrato runs into the Via dei Banchi Vecchi, which is the continuation of the old Via Peregrinorum. Instead, turn left just after the church and walk down Via della Barchetta. This brings you out into the:

13. **Via Giulia,** named for Pope Julius II, who commissioned the architect Bramante to create the first two straight thoroughfares in Rome, parallel but on opposite sides of the river (the other is Via della Lungara; see Walking Tour 7). The pope had a grand plan for this essentially circular design, which was never completed—at its northwest

end, the bridge that would have connected Via Giulia with Via della Lungara was never built. His plan to move major Vatican offices here, such as the papal tribunal, also never materialized. It is a grand street just the same, and is especially nice for walking now because it has been made a pedestrian-only zone.

Cross the Via Giulia and take the little Via San Eligio, which leads, on the left, to:

14. **Sant'Eligio degli Orefici,** a church that was designed by Raphael and begun in 1509 when the artist was 26 (he died in 1520). The facade collapsed in 1601, and was redone by Flaminio Ponzio and later architects of the 17th century (it wasn't finally finished until 1775).

On the same street, be sure to notice the **14th-century house** at number 7–8, one of the oldest remaining structures in the area and one of the few medieval dwellings (as opposed to churches) remaining in Rome. Then return to the Via Giulia and turn right again. You'll reach:

15. **Santa Maria dell'Orazione e Morte,** a church decorated in the late baroque style and possessing a somewhat ghoulish past. "Morte" means death, and this was the church of a society, the Compagnia della Morte, which was responsible for collecting unburied corpses. This was, of course, a religious charity rather than a "company" that gave decent burial to those—especially in the countryside—who had succumbed to disease, drowning, and other misfortunes. The bodies were interred underneath the church, and some still remain with handwritten cards describing where the body was found.

Continue on Via Giulia; presently you will pass behind the Palazzo Farnese, walking under what must be the most elegant overpass ever built: This is the private **"Via Farnesiorum,"** which originally allowed the Farnese family to walk from the Palazzo Farnese to their other palace across the river in Trastevere, the Farnesina (see Walking Tour 7, Part 2). Next on the right you will see the:

16. **Fontana del Mascherone,** a fountain erected in 1626, with an antique granite basin and above it a relief sculpture of a face with an open mouth. The story goes that on

holidays the Farnese family arranged for the fountain to pour wine, a free gift to the populace.

Shortly after passing the fountain, take the street on your left, the Vicolo del Polverone. This will bring you out into the Piazza della Quercia; turn right, and you will be standing in front of the:

17. **Palazzo Spada.** This beautiful palace was built in 1548–50 and is named for cardinal Bernardino Spada, who acquired it from another cardinal (Girolamo Capodiferro) and had it renovated by Borromini. The facade features beautiful stucco work by Giulio Mazzoni. The second floor has eight niches between the windows containing busts of famous Romans, including Romulus, Augustus, and Julius Caesar. The building is now property of the state and is the seat of the Consiglio (council of ministries), but you can enter the courtyard, where the rich decoration continues. On the left, in front of the library (enclosed by a glass window) is the famous **perspective gallery** of Borromini, a clever three-dimensional study in perspective that fools the eye. What appears to be a very long corridor of columns with a statue at the end is, in actuality, only 9m (less than 30 ft.) long with a statue that is waist high. By having the floor rise and the walls and ceiling slope in and downward, Borromini created a three-dimensional *trompe l'oeil.*

At the back of the courtyard you will see a sign for the **Galleria Spada** (© **06/6832409**), a wonderful collection of paintings and objects collected by Cardinal Bernardino and his relatives. The works are still displayed in Renaissance style, which means they are hung floor-to-ceiling amid the other period furnishings. Among the painters represented are Guido Reni, Guercino, Tiziano, and two women, Lavinia Fontana and Artemesia Gentileschi. Admission is charged.

Exiting the palazzo's courtyard, turn right on Via Capo di Ferro. On the right you will come to the church of:

18. **Santa Trinità dei Pellegrini,** which was built in 1558 for a society of pilgrims but later redone in baroque style. The interior contains some work by the important painters Guido Reni and Cavalier d'Arpino.

Continuing on, the street turns into the Via di S. Paolo alla Regola, at the end of which is the:

19. **Casa di San Paolo,** a house dating from the 13th century and one of the best examples of medieval architecture in Rome. The attached tower with the loggia at the top is particularly lovely. The house is named after a nearby church.

Turning to your left, you will find yourself in front of:

20. **Santa Maria in Monticelli.** This church, in need of restoration, appears at first glance to be relatively recent. In fact it is very ancient; the original church was restored in 1101 and has been restored many more times since then. Some of its older pieces remain, including a painting by Antonio Carracci, part of a 12th-century mosaic, and a 14th-century crucifix.

Continue on the short Via della Seggiola to the right of the church.

☕ **Take a Break** You can stop for one of the best homemade ice creams in Rome at **Pica,** at Via della Seggiola 12. Or enjoy coffee or another drink at the bar.

Via della Seggiola connects to the:

21. **Via Arenula,** a broad street opened in 1886–88. To the right, it leads to Trastevere; to the left, it ends at Largo di Torre Argentina. Turning left, you immediately enter the small park of Piazza Cairoli, with a small fountain and benches. At the far end is the church of San Carlo ai Catenari, built in the early 17th century.

At the left side of the piazza is the:

22. **Via de' Giubbonari,** which was part of the ancient Via Peregrinorum, the pilgrims' route. It is named for the sellers of *giubbe,* or jackets. Today it is lined with shops of all kinds, including gourmet Italian groceries and clothing and shoe stores, all the way up to where it disembogues into the Campo de' Fiori.

Continue straight ahead on Via Arenula and you will come to Largo di Torre Argentina, your starting point.

The Ghetto

Start: Piazza d'Aracoeli, off Piazza Venezia.

Finish: Piazza d'Aracoeli.

Time: 2 hours.

Best Time: Monday through Saturday from 8am to 1pm and from 4 to 7pm, when most of the palaces are open. The Crypta Balbi is closed on Mondays.

Worst Time: Lunch recess, when some of the palaces are closed, and Mondays if you want to visit the Crypta Balbi.

$$D$$uring the Middle Ages, Rome became the capital of a catholic religious state; while pagan cults had been outlawed in A.D. 390, well before the fall of the Roman Empire, the Jewish religion had never been a target of political action, and Rome counted a largish Jewish population among its citizens. As the popes consolidated their power over the city in the 13th century, however, they also started to transfer Jewish families into the Rione Sant'Angelo, the neighborhood near the Tiberina island and across from Trastevere. The neighborhood of Sant'Angelo, connecting the fords on the Tiber with the city markets and the area of the Fori, had great importance in Roman times, and was the location of

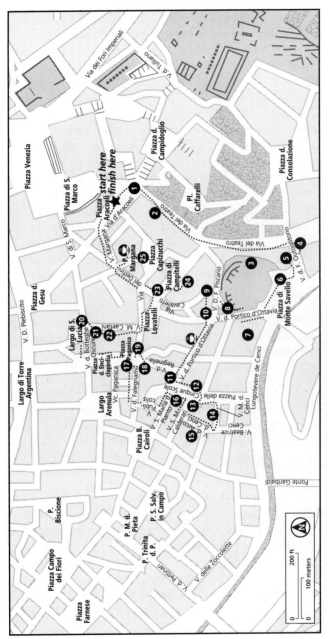

an amphitheater (the Circus Flaminius), and several theaters (Teatro Marcello and Teatro di Balbo), but it lost its predominance in medieval times. In 1555, Pope Paolo IV issued a law establishing a ghetto in the area of the Circus Flaminius, similar to the one that had been created in Venice a few years earlier. The area was surrounded by walls and all Roman Jews were forced to reside there. As its population grew, the area became extremely crowded; narrow roads were lined with seven-story buildings. The wave of urban renewal of the 15th, 16th, and 17th centuries did not affect Sant'Angelo and the ghetto, and the 19th century found the neighborhood basically untouched (with the exception of Piazza Campitelli).

With the new century, the ghetto doors were removed and in 1848 Pope Pius IX removed the residential restrictions. After 1870 and Italian unification, the whole area started undergoing great changes. The actual ghetto was completely demolished and replaced (with the new synagogue and three anonymous blocks of buildings), while the Teatro Marcello was isolated by demolishing all surrounding structures. Yet more buildings were demolished for the construction of Via del Teatro Marcello. Much remains to be seen today, however, as you will discover during our walk.

• • • • • • • • • • • • • • • • •

Start in Piazza d'Aracoeli, off Piazza Venezia to the right of the monument to Vittorio Emanuele II. You can easily get there by bus (a huge number of buses transit here; the most useful might be numbers 62, 64, 70, 81, 87, 492, or the electric minibus 119).

1. **Piazza d'Aracoeli.** Until 1928, this was a lively piazza surrounded by elegant palaces and hosting an outdoor food market. Then the piazza's entire eastern side was demolished to make room for the Via del Teatro Marcello. One church and two medieval towers were torn down. On the surviving sides of the piazza you can see the 16th century **Palazzo Muti Bussi** to the northwest, which was designed by Giacomo della Porta with a hexagonal plan and horseshoe-shaped courtyard (the fountain in front of the entrance is also designed by della Porta). To the south—actually at number 3 of Via della Tribuna di Tor de' Specchi—is a medieval tower which was transformed

into a house, and, nearby at number 3 of the square is **Palazzo Pecci Blunt.** This palace—formerly Palazzo Ruspoli—was also designed by Giacomo della Porta at the end of the 16th century; notice the richly decorated frieze and entablature around the facade. Next to it, at number 1, is the 17th-century **Palazzo Massimo di Rignano** by Carlo Fontana, graced by a Bernini-style fountain in the courtyard—also by Fontana. Incidentally, this is not the only place in Rome where you find these two artists paired; della Porta and Fontana together were responsible for completing St. Peter's after Michelangelo's death. (Notice the eastern corner of the building: It was cut away for the opening of Via del Teatro Marcello.)

Descend Via del Teatro Marcello; at number 40 you will find the entrance to the:

2. **Monastery of Tor de' Specchi.** Founded in 1433 by Santa Francesca Romana in a private house, the monastery was then extended to include the nearby medieval tower— Tor de' Specchi (tower of the mirrors)—so called because of the shape of its windows. Near number 34 you can see the remains of a medieval portico; the marble oval carving of Francesca Romana with an angel was salvaged from one of the demolished houses nearby. The monastery is open to the public only on March 9 and the following Sundays of that month; if you happen to be there at the right time it is well worth a visit, as the interior is decorated by 15th-century frescoes, including a beautiful one by Antoniazzo Romano right at the beginning of the Scala Santa.

Keep descending Via del Teatro Marcello, admiring the 12 surviving arches of the:

3. **Teatro Marcello.** Inaugurated in 11 B.C., this theater could hold 15,000 spectators. It was a favorite of ancient Romans and renowned for the quality of its performances, which included plays, tragedies, pantomimes, and what must have been the equivalent of cabaret, with music and singers. Romans apparently came here not only to hear music and poetry but also to find a mate or lover. The poet Ovid talks about Teatro Marcello in his *Ars Amatoria* (Art of Love) as one of the best places to go for romantic purposes. His audacious manual written in 2 B.C. explains the best tricks to secure (and keep) a lover.

Indeed, the theatre then must have been much like a popular theater in the 19th century, with the inevitable background of love stories with actresses and starlets. Abandoned in the 5th century, it became partly buried. The theater was then used as a source of construction materials before being turned into a fortified building and later a palace (Palazzo Orsini; see stop 6). It was excavated and restored in 1926–32, but the price was the surrounding medieval buildings which were demolished; 12 of the original arches from its eastern side remain, while the arches on its north side were rebuilt in tufa stone at the time of restoration.

Adjacent to the theater is a small archaeological area where you can see three marble columns supporting a decorative fragment; these were part of the very ancient **Temple of Apollo Sosiano,** built in 431 B.C. and restored in 179 B.C. Behind it is the medieval **Albergo della Catena** and to the east the platform of another temple.

Continue down Via del Teatro Marcello. You will pass (on your right) the imposing public building of the Anagrafe (civil registration)—a perfect example of architecture from the Fascist period. You will then come to a cross street; on your right it is called Via del Foro Olitorio, and on your left it is called Vico Jugario. Turn right and you will quickly reach the remains of the:

4. **Foro Olitorio,** the ancient Roman vegetable market that occupied the whole area from the slopes of the Campidoglio and the Teatro Marcello to the banks of the Tiber. It was composed of a large square paved in travertine marble and enclosed by buildings and temples.

Along Vico Jugario you can see a medieval house with its tower, and an archeological garden, the **Area Sacra di Sant'Omobono.** Here are remains of a **portico** and walls that were part of the Foro Olitorio, and a sacred area including two temples dating back to the 7th century B.C. The church across Via del Teatro Marcello at the corner of Via del Foro Olitorio is:

5. **San Nicola in Carcere,** built around the 7th century inside three early Roman temples that lined the Foro Olitorio—the Temple of Janus (on the left), the Temple

of Hope (in the middle), and the Temple of Juno Sospita (on built in the 3rd c. B.C., on the right). You can still see rows of columns and sections of the podium incorporated into the walls. The church was renovated in the 12th century and restored several times; the current facade is by Giacomo della Porta and dates from 1599. The buildings that surrounded it were demolished in 1934, isolating the church and restoring the medieval bell tower (the bell itself is an original from 1286).

Take Via del Foro Olitorio to:

6. **Piazza di Monte Savello,** which takes its name from the hill created by the ruined scene of the Teatro Marcello (see above). In medieval times, its ruined facade was used to build the fortified palace **Palazzo Orsini,** named after its last occupants who took it over in 1716. Notice the heraldic carvings of bears by the entrance at no. 30 Via Monte Savello, running along the north side of the square (*orsi* in Italian means "bears"). The oldest part of the building on the river side—also built directly on the arches of the theater—is hidden behind 19th-century additions.

Turn right onto Via del Portico d'Ottavia; this street once marked the northeastern limit of the ghetto. To your left is the:

7. **New Synagogue,** built between 1899 and 1904. It occupies 1 of the 4 blocks that replaced the ghetto. Inside is the **Museo dell'Arte Ebraica,** with a collection of archeological findings, together with interesting prints and religious items. It is open Sunday to Friday from 9am to 5pm in winter; in summer Monday to Thursday 9am to 7:30pm, Friday 9am to 1:30pm, and Sunday 9am to noon. Admission is charged.

Across, at number 29, is the:

8. **Casa dei Vallati,** from the 15th century (with additions from the 16th). It too was "liberated" from attached buildings during the excavations of the Teatro Marcello (see stop 3).

Just past it is the archaeological area of the:

9. **Portico d'Ottavia.** This is one of the most picturesque corners of Rome. It was an important passage between the

Forum and the area of the theaters in Roman times. It was built in 146 B.C. but redone in 27 B.C. by Augustus, who dedicated it to his sister, Octavia. It was restored in A.D. 203. This double portico encloses the Temple of Juno the Queen, the temple of Jupiter, and, to the north, Octavia's library, and is richly decorated with works of art. Throughout the Middle Ages and the Renaissance and up until the demolition of the ghetto in the 19th century, the portico was used as a fish market—probably one of the most elegant in the world!

Part of the portico was transformed into the church of:

10. **Sant'Angelo in Pescheria,** which has its facade inserted in the colonnade of the portico. The church gives its name to the neighborhood—Rione Sant'Angelo—and was built around 755. The interior was renovated in the 15th century. In the first chapel to the left you can admire a crucifix from the 16th century and in the second chapel to the left a fresco of the Madonna with Child and angels attributed to Benozzo Gozzoli, an associate and collaborator of Fra Angelico.

Take a Break **Giggetto al Portico d'Ottavia** (Via del Portico d'Ottavia 21/a) is an obvious stop for lunch or dinner. This historical restaurant has been serving delicious Roman Jewish cuisine for over a century and is always a local favorite (call for reservations at ℂ **06/ 6861105**); if you want just a snack instead, you can have some excellent take-away pizza at **Pizza Rustica** (Via del Portico d'Ottavia 5).

Continuing on Via del Portico d'Ottavia you'll find, at number 25, the **Torre dei Grassi** from the 13th century and, at numbers 8 and 13, the **houses of the Fabi** from the 15th and 16th centuries (notice the elegant windows on the second floor). Past Via di Sant'Ambrogio, Via della Reginella opens to your right; you can stroll along this narrow street to get an idea of what the old ghetto felt like. At the corner of Via della Reginella and Via del Portico d'Ottavia, is the:

11. **Casa dei Manili.** This interesting house was built by its owner, Lorenzo Manili, in 1468. He was a great admirer

of antiquity, as shown by the beautiful collection of archaeological fragments inserted in the walls of his house and by the date of construction carved on the building—year 2221, measured from the foundation of Rome and using the ancient Roman calendar.

Turn left on:

12. **Piazza delle Cinque Scole.** This is the location of the old synagogue, as well as ghetto's main entrance. The piazza takes its name from the five schools of the old temple—Scola del Tempio, Scola Castigliana, Scola Siciliana, Scola Nova, and Scola Catalana. The fountain on the square is by Giacomo della Porta; it decorated Piazza Giudea at the entrance of the old ghetto.

The western side of the square is graced by the:

13. **Palazzo Cenci Bolognetti.** This 15th-century palace is the main building of the so called **Isola dei Cenci (Island of the Cenci).** This complex of houses was the headquarters of the family Cenci, important in Rome already in the Middle Ages. The buildings were constructed, in part, over a hill made up of Roman ruins—the so-called Monte dei Cenci—which gives the name to the side street to the left of the square. Shelley was inspired by the legendary Beatrice Cenci, a protofeminist heroine who killed her depraved and abusive father (and was executed for it); she is the subject of his play *The Cenci.*

Turn right into:

14. **Via Monte de' Cenci.** To your right is the facade of Palazzo Cenci Bolognetti (above) and to your left is the chapel of **San Tommaso ai Cenci,** which was built over the ruins of the Temple of the Dioscuri and redone in the 16th century.

Turn right onto Via Beatrice Cenci to reach:

15. **Piazza Cenci,** the heart of the Isola dei Cenci. Here is the rear facade of Palazzo Cenci Bolognetti (above) at numbers 7 and 7A, and **Palazzetto Cenci** at number 56, built in the 16th century. You can enter in the courtyard and admire the elegant portico. To the right of the Palazzetto is the medieval **Arco dei Cenci.**

Take Via dell'Arco dei Cenci to the right and walk around the north side of the Isola dei Cenci, turning right again onto Via Santa Maria de' Calderari. At the corner where the street ends in Piazza delle Cinque Scole, at number 23B, you'll see the remains of a **monumental Roman portico,** with two half-columns and a brick arch.

Turn left onto Via Santa Maria del Pianto where, to your left, is the entrance of:

16. **Santa Maria del Pianto.** This church celebrates a miracle that occurred in the nearby Portico d'Ottavia in 1546, when an image of the Madonna painted on its walls was seen crying after a crime was committed under it. The sacred fresco is now venerated over the main altar of this church.

Further along to your right opens Via in Publicolis. At the corner, at number 43, is Rome's only example of *bugnato a punta di diamante* (a rare wall decoration technique known as "ashlar work," in which the stone blocks of the facade are beveled to a point) gracing the **Tower of Palazzo Santacroce,** redone in the 15th century.

Turn right onto Via in Publicolis, which, after a few steps, reaches Piazza Costaguti. Here you'll see the church of **Santa Maria in Publicolis,** belonging to the family Santacroce, and the side of Palazzo Costaguti (see below). Continue on, turning on Via dei Falegnami to your right, where you can admire a 15th-century portal at number 73. At the end of the street is:

17. **Piazza Mattei** with its famous turtle fountain. This is the heart of the **Isola Mattei (Island Mattei),** the complex of buildings encompassed by Via Caetani, Via de' Funari, Via Paganica, and Via delle Botteghe Oscure and owned by the powerful noble Roman family Mattei.

Romans tell an interesting story about this elegant fountain. It is said that the duke who lived in the family palace—the one just behind the fountain—was about to marry when he gambled all his fortune and lost it overnight. His future father-in-law then canceled the wedding, but the duke decided to show him how powerful a Mattei was even without a dime, and had the fountain built overnight. The morning after, he invited his future bride and her father to his palace and pointed at the fountain from the best window, saying to them, "Here is what an impoverished Mattei can accomplish in a few hours." He got to marry the girl, but to forget his humiliation had the window walled up, as it still appears today. Another story suggests that the duke borrowed the fountain from a friend for whose palace it had been built, and the fountain was simply left there. Whatever the truth, the fountain is certainly one of the most graceful in Rome. It was designed by Giacomo della Porta in 1581, and the turtles should be by Bernini, except that after having been stolen several times—first in 1906, and last in 1981, when one of them disappeared for good—the original turtles were removed to the Capitoline Museums and replaced by these copies on the fountain.

At number 10 of the piazza is the 16th-century **Palazzo Costaguti,** while at numbers 17 through 19 is the:

18. **Palazzo di Giacomo Mattei.** This is the first of the palaces built by this powerful family and is composed of two buildings. The one on the right is from the 15th century—inside is a courtyard graced by a pretty loggia—and the one on the left was built in the 16th century, also around a courtyard with a portico.

Take Via Paganica into what is today called Piazza dell'Enciclopedia Italiana. At number 4 is the 16th-century:

19. **Palazzo Mattei di Paganica,** which since 1928 has been the seat of the Italian Encyclopedia. Opening onto an inner courtyard surrounded by an elegant portico with loggia, the palace was built in part over the Roman Teatro di Balbo, a theatre constructed in 13 B.C.

Continue on Via Paganica and turn right onto:

20. **Via delle Botteghe Oscure.** This street—enlarged in 1938 by tearing down its entire north side—takes its name ("of the Dark Shops") from the shops and workshops housed in the ruined Teatro di Balbo and in the **Crypta Balbi,** a large courtyard surrounded by porticoes attached to the theater. The whole area has been excavated—work is still ongoing—and has been opened to the public since 2000 as part of the Museo Nazionale

Romano. The visit to the underground archaeological area shows how the portico was progressively transformed during early and late medieval times. Entrance is at Via delle Botteghe Oscure 31 and there is an admission fee.

At number 32 is the entrance to:

21. **Palazzo Caetani,** built for Alessandro Mattei in 1564, but bearing the name of the family that acquired it in 1776.

Continue on Via delle Botteghe Oscure and turn right in Via M. Caetani where, at number 32, is the entrance to:

22. **Palazzo Mattei di Giove,** started in 1598 by Carlo Maderno, and finished in 1618; this is the last addition to the Isola Mattei. Richly decorated inside, the palace is home to paintings by Domenichino, Pietro da Cortona, and others; it is also the seat of several offices, among which is the Library of Modern and Contemporary History.

Turn left on Via dei Funari; past the 16th-century facade of the church of **Santa Caterina dei Funari**—replacing the previous church of Santa Maria Dominae Rosae from the 12th century—is the Piazza Lovatelli. Here at number 1 is Palazzo Lovatelli, probably another of Giacomo della Porta's works, built around 1580. A few steps ahead is:

23. **Piazza Campitelli.** This scenic square—graced by another of Giacomo della Porta's fountains—is lined with palaces. At number 1 is the 16th-century **Palazzo Cavalletti,** at number 2 is **Palazzo Albertoni** from the 17th century, and at number 3 another 16th-century palace, **Palazzo Capizucchi.** The building at number 6 is modern, but it is graced by the facade of the **casa di Flaminio Ponzio,** originally built by this architect for himself in 1600 in Via Alessandrina, but moved here after the house was demolished to make way for the Via dei Fori Imperiali. (Another of these odd reconstructions is on Via Montanara—the continuation of Piazza Campitelli—where the church of Santa Rita da Cascia was put up after having been taken down in 1933 from its

original location to the left of the steps leading to Santa
Maria in Aracoeli.)

The church on the piazza is:

24. **Santa Maria in Campitelli,** the baroque masterpiece
of Carlo Rainaldi. Inside, over the main altar at the center of a baroque construction, is the miraculous image of
Santa Maria in Portico, a precious work of gilt and enam-
el from the 11th century. The *Madonna* is said to have liberated Rome from the plague that held the city in 1656,
and the church was built in her honor.

Take Via Cavalletti to the north, where at number 2 is
the 16th-century **Palazzo Clementi.** Continue on Via de'
Delfini, lined with 15th-century houses at numbers 29
through 31. The street opens into:

25. **Piazza Margana,** the medieval square created with the
construction of the **Torre dei Margani,** at number 40A,
one of Rome's few remaining examples of a fortified
medieval house.

☕ **Take a Break** You can gather the makings for an
excellent picnic at the **Pizzicheria de Santis** (Via
dei Delfini 25), where you'll find fresh bread, cheese, and
other local specialties. If you prefer a real meal, you
should not miss the historical restaurant **Tormargana**
(Piazza Margana 37; ✆ **06/69200493**) for a delicious
and scenic meal in this delightful square.

Continue on Via Margana where, fittingly, is the home
of Giacomo della Porta, the architect so active in this
neighborhood (at no. 14). Turn right onto Piazza
d'Aracoeli and you have finished this walking tour.

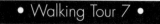

Trastevere

PART I

Start: Piazza Sonnino (tram 8 from Largo Argentina; bus 23, 630, or 780).

Finish: Piazza Santa Maria in Trastevere.

Time: 2½ hours, excluding time for visits.

Best Time: Monday through Saturday morning if you want to see the market of Piazza San Cosimato, also Monday through Saturday late afternoon if you don't care about the market and only want to visit the churches.

Worst Time: Sundays and the lunch lull when churches are closed to visitors.

O ne of Rome's most popular neighborhoods for its nightlife and great restaurants, Trastevere is also sought after for the special atmosphere of its narrow streets and medieval buildings. The neighborhood got its start in early Roman times with the development of the harbor on the opposite side of the river. It was also a residential

100

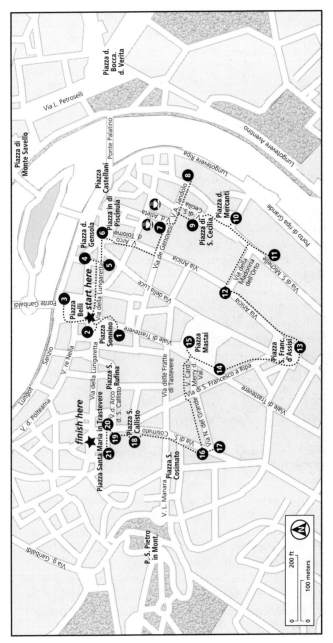

area for various groups of foreigners, including a large colony from Judea. Trastevere was enclosed in the city walls and the Janiculum Hill (*Gianicolo* in Italian) was an important defensive stronghold; however, the neighborhood always kept a separate character from the rest of Rome. Elegant patrician villas and gardens occupied parts of the Tiber's shore and the slopes of the Janiculum, while—as in other suburban areas—the river bend and lowlands subject to flooding were occupied by less expensive housing.

Mostly likely due to the composition of its population—the large colony of Judeans, in particular—Christianity developed here earlier than in the rest of the city. It is not by chance that the popes first established their power on this side of the river, while the rest of Rome remained in the hands of the civilian (and pagan) administration. Trastevere suffered semi-abandonment at the end of the Roman Empire, but the creation of the Vatican and of the Borgo (see Walking Tour 8) promoted the development neighborhood again, and in the 11th century it once again began to flourish.

Situated on the bank of the Tiber opposite the center of Rome, Trastevere developed its own dialect and customs, which caused a strong rivalry between the people of Trastevere (the last administrative subdivision of Rome) and the people of Monti (the neighborhood in the center of Rome, and the first administrative subdivision). Interestingly, our modern world *rivalry* comes from *riva,* the Latin word for *shore.* Each year the two factions confronted each other in a bloody fight, the *sassaiola* (see Walking Tour 1); this tradition began in the early Middle Ages and continued well into the 19th century.

The departure of the popes for Avignon in the 14th century brought the construction of new buildings to an abrupt halt; in the meantime, the Jewish community expanded. The return of the church ended this growth, and Jewish families began moving across the Tiber. In 1555, under the reign of Pope Paul IV, the Jewish population was segregated in the Ghetto (see Walking Tour 6), and of the many synagogues that once existed in Trastevere, only one remains today (see stop 7, Vicolo dell'Atleta).

This popular neighborhood in the bend of the river was little affected by the boom in construction and renovation during the Renaissance. Trastevere remained virtually untouched until the end of the 19th century, when the opening of Viale Trastevere and of the Lungotevere over the new river embankments maimed several areas. The opening of Viale Trastevere was particularly momentous as it cut off the southern half of the historical heart of the neighborhood. This area revived somewhat only in recent times, when restaurants, clubs, craft shops, and artists' studios and showrooms started spilling over from the more lively area around Piazza Santa Maria in Trastevere, on the northern side of the Viale. In spite of all this, Trastevere is the neighborhood of Rome that has best retained its authenticity, making it a neighborhood of unique charm.

This first part of our itinerary will take you through the medieval heart of Trastevere, where most of the paleo-Christian churches of Rome have been preserved.

● ● ● ● ● ● ● ● ● ● ● ● ● ● ● ● ●

Start in Piazza Sonnino. On the square (to your right if you have your back to the Tiber) is the church of:

1. **San Crisogono (St. Chrysogonus).** In the 12th century, Cardinal Giovanni da Crema had the 5th-century basilica that stood here destroyed and buried under his new creation. The facade bears the heraldic symbols of the Borghese family—dragons and the eagles—in memory of Cardinal Scipione Borghese, who had the church restored in the early 17th century. The bell tower from the 12th century was then topped with a peaked roof, while the interior was decorated with stucco and a coffered wooden ceiling. At the center of the ceiling is the *Glory of St. Crisogono.* The original was painted by Guercino but was stolen in 1808; it is now in London, at Stafford House. The church is full of works of art, from the 13th-century cosmatesque floor, to the 13th-century mosaic in the apse, to the numerous 17th-century paintings. Under the church are the remains of the paleo-Christian basilica, with some beautiful frescoes from the 11th century (you access these from the sacristy).

To the right of San Crisogono opens the small square Largo San Giovanni de' Matha. Here you find the church of:

2. **Sant'Agata.** Another early church—probably from the 11th century—it was rebuilt in the 17th century and restored in the 19th. Its real point of interest is the image of the Madonna to the left of the main altar. This is **Madonna de' Noantri,** the patroness of Trastevere who is celebrated in a traditional festivity—the *Festa de' Noantri*—in July. Although the religious element of the celebrations has somewhat tapered off in modern times in favor of other events including concerts and shows, this church and its Madonna are still at the center of it all and much venerated in the neighborhood.

Continue toward the Tiber where at the head of the Ponte Garibaldi is:

3. **Piazza Belli,** dedicated to the Roman poet Giuseppe Gioacchino Belli, who wrote in the local dialect; his statue at the center of the square is from 1913. To the northwest is **Palazzetto Anguillara,** a medieval palace with a tower from the 13th century—**Torre dell'Anguillara.** The palace was renovated and enlarged in the 15th century, and was substantially modified again to accommodate the opening of Viale Trastevere; the medieval tower, however, is untouched.

Retrace your steps by walking away from the Tiber, and turn left onto Via della Lungaretta; this street was opened in the 16th century over the ancient Roman *Aurelia Vetus.* To your left is:

4. **Vicolo della Luce** with, at the corner, a well-preserved 14th-century house. This building is very unusual for Rome, where houses from that period have virtually disappeared. It is graced by Gothic arches and an external staircase.

Continue on Via della Lungaretta and turn right into Via della Luce. Here you'll see:

5. **Santa Maria della Luce,** a church that dates from the 3rd or 4th century A.D. It was renovated in the 12th century, and now hides behind a 19th-century facade. The

interior was also redone in the 19th century, but if you turn right again around the church on Vicolo del Buco, you can see the original medieval transept.

Return to Via della Lungaretta and continue on to:

6. **Piazza in Piscinula** where, to your left, is the 14th-century **Palazzo Mattei,** restored at the beginning of the 20th century; and, to your right, the 19th-century facade of **San Benedetto in Piscinula.** The church was built in the 11th century around the cell of the saint—which you can still visit (access from the Chapel of the Madonna, as you enter the church to the left)—and finished in the 12th century.

Take Via Arco dei Tolomei, past Palazzo Mattei to your left, and, passing under the **Medieval arch** of the house of the Tolomei (a Sienese family that moved here in the 14th c.), onto Via Anicia. Turn left onto Via dei Genovesi and again left into:

Take a Break If you want to sample the local nightlife, try the Greek **Ouzerie** (Via dei Salumi 2) where you can have a light meal and listen to live music on Fridays and Saturday nights.

Take a Break If you like ice cream, do not miss the homemade *gelato* of the **Gelateria alla Scala** (Via della Scala 5), one of the best—and most generously sized servings—in Rome.

7. **Vicolo dell'Atleta.** This picturesque alley is named after a statue found here in the 19th century and now in the Vatican Museums. Trastevere was once the seat of an important colony of Judeans that first arrived during ancient Roman Republic. This neighborhood was home to many synagogues, but the only remaining medieval synagogue is here at number 14 Vicolo dell'Atleta. You can still see an inscription in Hebrew carved on the central column of the arches. Further on, at numbers 2 and 3–4, are two houses dating from the Renaissance.

Return to Via dei Genovesi, admiring the other Renaissance home at numbers 9–10, and continue on through the next intersection to the end of Via Augusto

Jandolo. Here, inside the courtyard of the hospital by the same name is the church of:

8. **Santa Maria in Cappella.** This diminutive church was consecrated in the year 1090 as is stated on a marble plaque inside. The church was restored in the 19th century—which is the date of the new facade—but the bell tower is still the original from the 12th century.

Retrace your steps to the intersection and turn left onto Via di Santa Cecilia, which, after a few steps, opens into Piazza di Santa Cecilia. Here to your right is the basilica of:

9. **Santa Cecilia in Trastevere.** This church was built in the 9th century over the Roman house venerated since the 5th century as the home of Saint Cecilia and her husband, Saint Valeriano. The portico, bell tower, and right wing of the monastery with the cloister were added at the end of the 12th century and can still be seen behind the 18th-century monumental facade of the complex. The apse of the church is still decorated with the original mosaics from 820, while the ciborium over the main altar is a masterpiece by Arnolfo di Cambio, from 1293—you can still see his signature next to the date. Under the main altar is another famous masterpiece, the portrait of the body of Saint Cecilia by Carlo Maderno, completed in 1600. The origin of this work of art is somewhat creepy: Cardinal Paolo Emilio Sfondrati requested the recognition of the body of the saint, which was exhumed in 1599, and Maderno depicted it as it was seen on that occasion. The inner facade of the church houses the choir of the nuns, which was added in the 16th century, covering the magnificent frescoes painted by Pietro Cavallini between 1289 and 1293. These were rediscovered in 1900 and it is now possible to admire them by climbing the staircase to the choir.

Continue past the church to:

10. **Piazza dei Mercanti.** This is one of the most picturesque squares in Trastevere and is lined with houses typical of the neighborhood. At number 19 (on the corner with Piazza di Santa Cecilia), is another original medieval

house; this one was restored in 1960. Also on the square is one of the historical restaurants of Rome, **Meo Patacca,** famous for its typical Roman fare, histrionics, and minstrels that enliven the meal and can be quite a source of amusement for the diners.

Take Via di San Michele; the building to your left is the:

11. **Ex Ospizio Apostolico di San Michele a Ripa Grande,** today housing the Ministry of Cultural Heritage. Created in the 17th century as a conservatory for boys, other institutions were later attached to it, including a hospice for the elderly, a reformatory for boys, a home for unmarried women, and finally a prison for women. This last remained in use until 1970.

Retrace your steps and turn onto Via della Madonna dell'Orto. At the end of the street you will see the scenic facade of a church, unfortunately somewhat suffocated by a building surrounding it on both sides, the Manifattura di Tabacchi (see Piazza Mastai, stop 15). The church is:

12. **Santa Maria dell'Orto.** This graceful church—a beautiful example of Roman baroque—was built around a 15th-century chapel housing the venerated image of the Madonna, detached from the walls of a vegetable garden nearby (the work is still preserved over the main altar). Inside the church is a collection of paintings from the 16th through the early 18th centuries, when the church was finally finished. Construction was slow because the church was done by the *Arcciconfraternita,* an association of the guilds of a variety of occupations—including *pollaroli* (poultry sellers) and *pizzicaroli* (sellers of cheese and cured meat)—which are still represented in the small museum above the church.

Turn left on Via Anicia and follow it to Piazza San Francesco d'Assisi where, to your left, is the church and convent of:

13. **San Francesco a Ripa.** This church was built over the church of San Biagio and a Benedictine monastery where St. Francis stayed. The Franciscans took over the church in the 13th century and completely renovated it. The church was later enlarged, and then it was rebuilt in the

17th century. In 1873 most of the convent was turned into barracks and stayed that way until 1943. Inside is one of Bernini's masterpieces, the statue of the **Beata Ludovica Albertoni,** in the chapel of the left transept.

Take Via di San Francesco a Ripa, opened at the beginning of the 17th century to connect this church with Santa Maria in Trastevere (see later) and turn right into:

14. **Viale di Trastevere.** Originally named Viale del Re, this tree-lined alley—in typical French and Piemontese tradition—was created to connect the center of Rome with the newly built train station of Trastevere nearby. It cut through the historical neighborhood, destroying the continuity of the urban fabric and isolating its southern half from the more commercial areas to the north.

To your right opens:

15. **Piazza Mastai.** This square was the heart of a new development—the *quartiere Mastai*—created by Pope Pio IX Mastai in 1863. It encompassed a tobacco processing plant—the *Manifattura di Tabacchi*—closing the square to the east, and dwellings for the workers (one remains on the right of the hemicycle) surrounding it on the other sides. Many buildings were destroyed to make way for the Viale Trastevere, which opened in 1899; one can barely imagine what Piazza Mastai must have looked like with its western side intact. In 1958 the processing plant here was maimed when its two wings were demolished and replaced by modern—and ugly—buildings.

Take Via Cardinale Merry del Val, opening across from the factory, on the other side of Viale Trastevere. This street was the main access to the square and the *quartiere Mastai,* marked by the two majestic *propilei* (pillars) siding the street, which you can still see at the corner of Via San Francesco a Ripa. Cross this and take Via N. del Grande to:

16. **Piazza San Cosimato.** Lined with popular housing built in the 19th century and, to your left by the former monastery of San Cosimato (see below). This pleasant triangular space is home to one of Rome's historical outdoor food markets, a colorful experience and an excellent

source of picnic fare. It is open Monday through Saturday from 6am to 2pm.

Walk to number 76 to your left, where you will find the entrance to the complex of:

17. **San Cosimato.** Today a hospital (Ospedale Nuovo Regina Margherita), this monastery was established in the 10th century and enlarged in the 12th and again in the 15th century. It became a hospice in the 19th century and was modified accordingly. Entrance is through the first cloister, which dates from the 13th century; from there you can reach the courtyard and then the church. Built together with the convent in the 10th century, the church was also redone in later times; the Madonna over the main altar is from the 13th century and was moved here from the old basilica of St. Peter's. Attached to the first cloister is a second cloister from the 15th century.

Take Via di San Cosimato to:

18. **Piazza San Callisto.** This scenic little square is defined by the facade of **Palazzo Farinacci.** This elegant palace from the 16th century is connected to Palazzo Cavalieri (see Piazza Santa Maria in Trastevere, stop 20) by the **Arco di San Callisto,** a graceful passage over the street below. Passing under it, notice at number 42 of the appropriately named Via dell'Arco di San Callisto, one of the smallest buildings you'll see in Rome: a two-story diminutive house with an external staircase.

Also on the square is the church of:

19. **San Callisto,** built in the 8th century over the very spot where, the story goes, Saint Callisto died in martyrdom. This church was attached to the Benedictine monastery housed in the Palazzo di San Callisto (see below); both the church and the monastery were renovated in the 17th century. Walk inside the church and look in the right chapel: The two angels supporting a painting are by Giovanni Lorenzo Bernini.

Pass between the corners of the two palaces closing the square to the north to enter:

20. **Piazza Santa Maria in Trastevere,** the heart of Trastevere and a beautiful square, reorganized in the 17th

century around a fountain by Carlo Fontana. Entering the square, to your left is the **Palazzo di San Callisto**—a medieval palace renovated in the 17th century—which originally housed the monastery of the same name. To your right is the 16th century **Palazzo Cavalieri,** and across the square to the right of the church (see below) is the 18th century Casa dei Canonici.

The last side of the square is taken up by the basilica of:

21. **Santa Maria in Trastevere.** This was the first church dedicated to the cult of the Virgin Mary and probably the first official church in Rome. It was founded by Pope St. Callistus in the 3rd century over the *Taberna Meritoria,* a hospice for maimed soldiers. According to the legend, the Christians asked the emperor to give them the Taberna to built their first church because they considered it a holy place. Indeed, in 38 B.C., oil had suddenly spurted out of the ground in front of the Taberna, hence the name *fonte dell'olio* (oil spring) of the street to the right of the church. Early Christians interpreted this phenomenon as announcing the coming of Christ. A more secular explanation maintains that the name was not *fons olei* (oil spring) but *fons olidus* (polluted spring), from the aqueduct of gray waters Augustus used to flood the area for his *naumachiae* (boating games).

Whichever story is true, Pope Julius I transformed the church into a basilica in the 4th century. It was then rebuilt in the 12th century using marble from the Baths of Caracalla. Later additions and restorations have preserved the main body of the basilica, making it one of the most splendid 12th-century churches. The harmonious interior is particularly famous for the superb 12th-century **mosaics** in the apse—in a very good state of preservation—and the painting of the **Madonna** over the altar from the 6th century.

Piazza Santa Maria in Trastevere is the last stop of the first part of our walk. If you don't want to continue with the second part, turn your back to Santa Maria in Trastevere and cross the square to Via della Lungaretta. Piazza Sonnino, where you started and where you'll find public transportation, is only a few steps away.

PART II

Start: Piazza Santa Maria in Trastevere, at the end of Via della Lungaretta from Piazza Sonnino (tram 8 from Largo Argentina; bus 23, 630, or 780).

Finish: Piazza Sonnino.

Time: 2½ hours, excluding time for visits.

Best Time: Monday through Saturday morning if you want to visit Villa Farnesina; also Monday through Saturday late afternoons if you don't care about the Farnesina and only want to visit the churches.

Worst Time: Afternoon and Sunday, when the Villa Farnesina is closed; also Monday through Saturday during the lunch lull when churches are closed to visitors.

D uring the Renaissance, elegant gardens and villas started to be built on the slopes of the Janiculum and along the shore of the Tiber, following the same urbanization pattern from Roman times. The area to the north of Trastevere, squeezed between the Tiber and the steeper slope of the Janiculum Hill, was further developed in the Baroque period to strengthen the urban fabric connecting Trastevere to the Vatican. This is when the first of two long alleys that run through the neighborhood lengthwise—Via della Lungara by the Tiber—was opened. The second alley, the Passeggiata del Gianicolo at the top of the Janiculum Hill (see later) was opened much later, at the end of the 19th century.

This second part of our itinerary takes you through the northern half of Trastevere. Most of the walk takes place in the Renaissance area with its elegant villas, both along the Tiber and up the slopes of the Janiculum. You will also stroll the most typical and lively part of the medieval heart of the neighborhood, the river bend, which we began exploring in the first part of this itinerary.

• • • • • • • • • • • • • • • •

From Piazza Sonnino and with your back to the Tiber, take Via della Lungaretta to your right. Cross Piazza Santa Maria in Trastevere to Via della Paglia; this opens onto:

1. **Largo Fumasoni Biondi,** where you can see the transept of Santa Maria in Trastevere and the church's 12th-century bell tower. To the right, at numbers 4 and 5, is the facade of the **church's** *Canonica* (the priest's residence) in Borrominian style.

   Before the Canonica to your right is:

2. **Vicolo del Piede,** one of the most characteristic corners of the neighborhood and named for the marble foot (a fragment of an ancient Roman statue) lying there.

   Retrace your steps to Largo Fumasone Biondi, which opens to the right onto:

3. **Piazza Sant'Egidio.** This triangular space is named after the early-17th-century church of **Sant'Egidio** opening onto it. The convent to which the church belongs, also from the same period, is adjacent to the church. It houses the **Museo di Roma in Trastevere,** part of the Museum of Rome of Palazzo Braschi (see Walking Tour 2), and specializes in the social and folkloristic aspects of the city's culture. The life-size scenographies depicting life in Rome at the beginning of the 19th century are quite impressive, and so is the collection of watercolors, paintings, and prints of parts of central Rome that have now disappeared. At number 9 on the square is the 15th-century **Palazzo Velli,** while to the left is Vicolo del Cedro, climbing towards the Janiculum Hill (see later). On that street, immediately to your left at number 35, is an 18th-century house with great baroque windows.

   Take Via della Scala, which opens to the left onto Piazza della Scala. Here is the church of:

4. **Santa Maria della Scala,** which was built in the 16th century to house a miraculous image of the Madonna. Over the main altar by Carlo Rainaldi is a precious ciborium, and on the wall a *Madonna col Bambino* (Madonna with Baby) by the Cavalier d'Arpino from 1612. The chapel of the Madonna della Scala with the miraculous

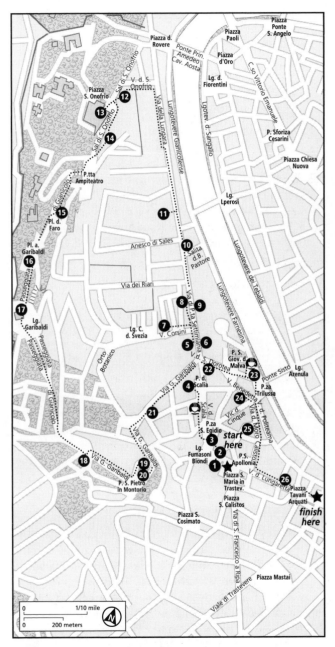

Piazza Ponte
S. Angelo

Piazza
Paoli

Piazza d.
Rovere

Piazza
d'Oro

Ponte Prin
Amedeo
Cav. Aosta

Lg. d.
Fiorentini

C.so Vittorio Emanuele

Lgotev. d. Sangallo

Piazza
S. Onofrio

V. d. S.
Onofrio

Sal. di S. Onofrio

Sal. di S. Onofrio

P. Sforiza
Cesarini

Piazza Chiesa
Nuova

Lg.
Lperosi

P.tta
Ampiteatro

di Gianicolo

Via della Lungara

Lungotevere Gianicolense

Lungotevere dei Tebaldi

Pl. d.
Faro

Pl. a.
Garibaldi

Anesco di Sales

Salita
d. B.
Pastore

Passeggiata Gianicolo

Lg.
Garibaldi

Via dei Riari

Lungotevere Farnesina

Passeggiata Passeggiata

Orto
Botanico

Lg. C.
d. Svezia

V. Corsini

V. di Via Settimania

V. d. S. Dorotea

P. S.
Giov. d.
Malva

Ponte Sisto

Lg.
Arenula

Passeggiata
di Gianicolo

Via G. Garibaldi

V. d.
Scalia

P. d.
Scalia

P.za
Trilussa

V. Benedetta

Via G. Garibaldi

V. d.
Scalia

Vic. d.
Cinque

Via d. Politeama

Via d. Moro

Via d. Pettinari

Via G. Garibaldi

P.za
S. Egidio

Lg.
Fumasoni
Biondi

*start
here*

P.S.
Apollonia

Via d. Lungaretta

P.za
Tavani
Arquati

P. S. Pietro
in Montorio

Piazza S. Maria in
Trastev.

Piazza
S. Calistos

*finish
here*

Piazza S.
Cosimato

Piazza di S. Francesco a Ripa

Viale di Trastevere

Piazza Mastai

0   1/10 mile

0   200 meters

Nightlife in Trastevere

In **Testaccio,** clubs come and go, but the neighborhood remains one of the preeminent Roman hot spots. **Club Picasso** (Via Monte Testaccio 63; ✆ **06/5742975;** Metro: B to Piramide) has blasting music—from rock to blues—for most of the night.

During the summer, the **Estate Romana** festival provides additional dancing venues, including on a barge on the Tiber and on the terraces and gardens of monuments around town.

Cover charges hover between 10€ and 20€ ($13–$26) for the most elegant and hippest venues. They usually open around 10:30pm and close around 4am.

image is in the left transept; its altar and the monument to the right are by Alessandro Algardi.

Continue on Via della Scala and pass under **Porta Settimiana,** a gate in the Aurelian walls rebuilt in the 15th century. Beyond, along Via di Porta Settimiana to your left, you encounter:

5. **Palazzo Torlonia.** This elegant palace was built in the 16th century for the powerful Roman family Torlonia. In the 19th century, Prince Alessandro Torlonia organized a museum here to house the family's rich private collection of antiquities—mostly sculptures and carvings. The museum, though, was later dismantled and the palace has been turned into apartments.

Past it is the beginning of the:

6. **Via della Lungara.** Opened by Julius II in 1508, this was the longest straight road of Renaissance Rome, connecting Trastevere with Borgo, the neighborhood around the Vatican (see Walking Tour 9). This street—together with Via Giulia (see Walking Tour 5)—was part of a project devised by Bramante to improve the circulation of traffic in the center of Rome. Along this street Rome's gentry built villas and gardens, some of which have been preserved to our day. Unfortunately, half of the buildings

on the right-hand side have been demolished to make way for the construction of the Tiber's new embankments and the Lungotevere.

The first street to your left is Via Corsini, where, at the end, is the entrance to the:

7. **Orto Botanico (Botanical Garden).** The origins of this garden go back to the Middle Ages in 1289, when Pope Nicholas III, following a longstanding tradition for monks, established a garden of decorative and medicinal plants inside the Vatican walls. In the 17th century, Pope Alexander VII decided to transfer the Vatican plants into the garden of the convent of San Pietro in Montorio (see below). There the garden thrived thanks to the dedicated care of the botanist Giovan Battista Trionfetti who, through exchanges with foreign experts, enlarged the collection to over 3,000 species. At his death in 1708, though, the garden entered a period of decline, which stopped only with the institution in 1820 of two chairs of botanical studies in the University of Rome and the assignment of the direction of the garden to one of them.

The garden—moved to the grounds of Palazzo Salviati (see below) in 1823—started recovering but in 1876 it was moved again, temporarily, across the Tiber. Finally, in 1883, the Orto found its permanent home in the gardens of Palazzo Riario Corsini. Covering about 12,000 sq. m (129,000 sq. ft.), it now numbers approximately 3,500 species. The oldest tree is the 400-year-old plane tree *(Platanus orientalis),* a plant introduced by the ancient Romans from the Middle East. It is open Monday through Saturday from 9am to 6pm in winter and until 7pm in spring and summer.

Retrace your steps and turn left onto Via della Lungare. At number 10 is:

8. **Palazzo Corsini,** built in 1510 for Cardinal Raffaele Riario, nephew of Sixtus IV. Bought by the Corsini in 1736 to house the family's library and picture gallery, it was then restored and enlarged. Sold to the Italian government in 1883, it now houses the Accademia dei Lincei (see Villa Farnesina, below) and the **Galleria Corsini.** This large collection includes a number of masterpieces

by Italian and foreign artists—Flemish and French among others—including Caravaggio's famous *San Giovanni Battista.* Open Tuesday to Sunday, from 8:30am to 1:30pm. Admission is charged.

Across from Palazzo Corsini is:

9. **Villa Farnesina.** This elegant villa was famous for its gardens and the loggia—designed by Raphael—which overlooked the Tiber. The loggia and part of the gardens were unfortunately destroyed during the construction of the new embankments of the Tiber in 1884. The villa is still well worth a visit for the magnificent frescoes by Raphael and his school that decorate the interior. Built in 1508 for the Sienese banker Agostino Chigi, the villa was abandoned at his death and bought by the Farnese (hence its name) in 1590. Passed to the Italian government in 1927, it was restored and now houses the reception halls of the **Accademia dei Lincei**—a major Italian cultural institute—and the **Gabinetto Nazionale delle Stampe,** the largest print collection in Italy. It is open Monday through Saturday from 9am to 1pm. Admission is charged.

Outside the Villa's walls, at the corner with Salita del Buon Pastore, are the remains of the **Scuderie Chigi,** the stables of the villa, designed by Raphael and demolished in 1808. Further on is the church of:

10. **San Giacomo in Settignano,** founded in the 9th century and renovated in the 17th. Inside is the tomb of **Ippolito Merenda** by Giovanni Lorenzo Bernini. The church's 13th-century bell tower—the only one from that period in Rome with a single arched opening—can be seen from the Lungotevere behind the church. From outside the church you can enjoy the best **view of Villa Lante** (see below), site of the Embassy of Finland to the Holy See, on the Janiculum Hill.

Beyond, the right side of Via della Lungara disappears, demolished for the opening of the Lungotevere, and across are the forbidding walls of the:

11. **Carcere giudiziario Regina Coeli,** the prison that was created in 1881 by connecting and modifying the two convents that existed there.

Continue on Via della Lungara, passing, at numbers 43 to 45, the convent and church of **San Giuseppe alla Lungara.** Built in the 18th century, it forms a continuum with the symmetrical building—by the same architect—at numbers 46 to 49. Beyond, at numbers 82 and 83 is **Palazzo Salviati,** built in 1520 by Giulio Romano. Take Via di Sant'Onofrio to your left. This climbs the slopes of the:

12. **Janiculum Hill (Gianicolo).** This hill derives its name from the cult of Janus, who in ancient Roman times most likely had an important temple here. Here Garibaldi strenuously defended the Roman republic in 1849 against the French troops that had come to restore the power of the pope.

    Turn left on Salita di Sant'Onofrio. In front of you are the church and convent of:

13. **Sant'Onofrio.** Built in the 15th century, the church is richly decorated with frescoes and stucco, including, in the first chapel to the right, an *Annunciazione* (Annunciation) by Antoniazzo Romano. The first chapel to the left is dedicated to Torquato Tasso, the famous Italian poet and author of the epic poem *Gerusalemme Liberata.* He died in the attached convent and was buried here in 1595. The votive lamp in Liberty style in the chapel is by Duilio Cambellotti, from 1928. Access to the convent is from the right of the church's portico; you can visit the 15th-century cloister and loggia with frescoes by the Cavalier d'Arpino. Inside the convent is the **Museo Tassiano,** dedicated to the poet.

    To the left of the church starts the:

14. **Passeggiata del Gianicolo.** This scenic promenade along the ridge of the hill was built in 1880 over the city's 17th-century walls.

    Skirting the Hospital of the Bambino Gesù (up to your right) the alley turns right and, right after the bend, you can take the ramp of stairs that climbs to your left. This is a pedestrian shortcut saving you a couple of long bends of the road. It leads to:

15. **Piazza del Faro.** An unlikely sight this far from the sea, the lighthouse was donated to Italy by the Italians of Argentina, in memory of their country of origin. From the terrace around it you can enjoy the famous **panorama,** encompassing the entire city.

    Continue on to the next terrace, with the:

16. **Monumento ad Anita,** the monument to Garibaldi's wife, his companion in fights and adventures (and under which she is buried). Across from her monument is **Villa Lante,** the 16th-century villa by Giulio Romano, built over the ruins of the ancient Roman villa of Marziale and now belonging to Finland.

    Following the alley lined with busts of Garibaldi's soldiers, you reach:

17. **Piazzale Giuseppe Garibaldi,** the main terrace at the top of the hill, dedicated to the hero of Italian *Risorgimento* (Resurgence) and graced by his statue. From here you can enjoy another excellent view over the city.

    Take the alley to the left, which descends to the:

18. **Fontana dell'Acqua Paola,** the fountain at the end of Trajan's aqueduct. During the Gothic Wars at the end of the Roman Empire, marauding Goths severed the aqueduct. The water flow was reactivated in 1612 by Pope Paul V after 4 years of work.

    Take Via Garibaldi to the right and descend to the panoramic terrace of:

19. **San Pietro in Montorio.** This church was built in the 9th century over what was then believed to be the place of martyrdom of St. Peter. The name "in Montorio" comes from the other ancient Roman name of the Janiculum, *Mons Aureus* (golden mountain), which derives from the yellow color of the earth that composes it. Rebuilt in the 15th century, the interior of the church is richly frescoed; the second chapel to the left is by Bernini.

    Attached to the church is the convent, which was rebuilt in the 16th century. Of the two cloisters, the first to the right of the church is graced by one of the most famous monuments of the Renaissance, the:

20. **Tempietto del Bramante.** The perfect visual balance of its architectural components and the harmonious use of central perspective make this small but elegant temple a model of 16th-century Roman architecture. Built around 1506, its floor is in cosmatesque style (mosaic of marble and colored stones). The double ramp of stairs descending to the crypt was added by Bernini in 1628. The center of the hole is thought to be the exact location where St. Peter was martyred on the cross.

Continue downhill on Via San Pietro in Montorio back to Via Giuseppe Garibaldi. After a bend to the right you'll pass the church of:

21. **Santa Maria dei Sette Dolori.** Continue down Via Garibaldi, passing, at numbers 41 to 45, the long facade of the ex-tobacco plant *(Fabbrica del Tabacco)*. This building was designed by Luigi Vanvitelli, the master of the splendid Reggia di Caserta (Caserta's Royal Palace) near Naples that was built in the 18th century. Renovated several times, the tobacco plant now houses the Carabinieri Officers' School.

Cross Via della Lungara into:

22. **Via di Santa Dorotea.** Here, at numbers 19A and 20, is a medieval house renovated in the 15th century. Tradition has it that this is the house of Margherita Liuti, Raphael's great love, whom he painted in his famous portrait, *La Fornarina,* now in the museum of Palazzo Barbarini. The painter had his home nearby on Via della Lungara.

Continuing on across Piazza San Giovanni della Malva and into Via di Ponte Sisto, you'll find yourself in:

23. **Piazza Trilussa.** This square was created at the end of the 19th century and dedicated to the Roman poet Trilussa, pseudonym of Carlo Alberto Salustri, whose bust is to your left. The great fountain to your right—today unfortunately used as a bath by groups of homeless—is the Fontanone dell'Acqua Paola from 1613. Until 1898 it was at the end of Via Giulia (see Walking Tour 5) on the opposite side of the river, but it was moved here after the opening of the Lungotevere.

Take the street to the left of the fountain and turn right on:

24. **Via Benedetta.** Here, at numbers 19, 20, and 21, are two 15th-century houses with the classic structure of the time: shops on the first floor and living quarters on the second. The houses are graced by elegant windows.

    Retracing your steps, cross Vicolo del Cinque into Via del Moro, and turn right into Vicolo de' Renzi. This leads to:

25. **Piazza de' Renzi,** another of the picturesque hidden spots of Trastevere. Here a two-story tall medieval house survives, virtually untouched.

    Take a Break If you are tired of Roman food, at **Surya Mahal** (Piazza Trilussa 50) you can have authentic Indian food in an upscale decor. If instead you prefer typical Roman fare, head for **Checco er Carrettiere** at Via Benedetta 10, or for the **Osteria Ponte Sisto** at Via Ponte Sisto 80, both off Piazza Trilussa.

    Retrace your steps to Via del Moro and continue on. Turn left into Via della Lungaretta. At the corner with Vicolo di Santa Rufina to your left is the:

26. **Bell tower of the church of Sante Rufina e Seconda.** This slender 12th-century tower is all you can see of the church, which in the 17th century was enclosed inside the convent of the same name. The church next to it is the 13th-century **Santa Margherita,** which was reoriented by 90 degrees when it was rebuilt in the 17th century.

    Continue on Via della Lungaretta, passing Piazza Tavani Arquati, maimed by the demolition of its northern side for the Lungotevere, to Piazza Sonnino.

The Vatican

Start: Metro stop Cipro–Musei Vaticani.

Finish: Metro stop Ottaviano.

Time: 1½ hours, excluding time for visits.

Best Time: Monday through Saturday, if you want to visit St. Peter's Basilica and the Vatican Museums.

Worst Time: Sunday morning during Mass, when visits are not allowed and the museums are closed.

D uring ancient Roman times, this section of Rome was a suburban area called the *Ager Vaticanus,* occupied by fields and large villas. Agrippina, the mother of Caligula, owned a large part of it, and this is probably why Caligula built his circus (or arena) here, which was later finished by Nero. That circus had a momentous bearing on the future of the area because it was probably there that Jesus' apostle Peter was executed. His body was buried nearby and immediately became the destination of pilgrimages by Christians. In A.D. 320, Emperor Constantine started building a basilica over Peter's tomb, which strengthened the appeal of the pilgrimage site. In the 7th and 8th centuries, organized groups of pilgrims started arriving from the north, giving birth to a permanent settlement around the basilica. Mainly Saxons, but also Lombards, Franks, and Frisians, they left several enduring signs of their presence, first of all in the name of the streets, called *borgo* from the Gothic word *burg*. Each group had its own small neighborhood with its own church, some of which are still standing.

The Saracens sacked the basilica in 846. Pope Leo IV decided to build a ring of walls around the area, completing that work in 852. In his honor, the neighborhood took the name *Città Leonina* (Leo's Town). In subsequent centuries, popes built heavily in the area, transforming Leo's Town into the official papal residency and thus the center of the Catholic Church. In 1305, however, escalating political tension in Italy spurred Pope Clement V to abandon the area. Taking his cardinals and court with him, Clement moved to Avignon in southern France. When the papacy returned to Rome in 1377, it found its buildings and palaces in ruins. The Renaissance popes of the 15th and 16th centuries were grand builders and great patrons of the arts. They rapidly rebuilt and renovated the area, and many cardinals built sumptuous palaces.

The popes also restored the walls, but these were not enough to prevent another sacking of the town in 1527. Paul III reinforced the walls, while Pius IV enlarged them to enclose a new neighborhood—called Borgo Pio in his honor—to the north of the *Città Leonina*.

Except for the substantial demolitions for the opening of Piazza San Pietro in the 17th century, the whole Vatican City remained untouched until the 20th century. Even the development of the neighborhood of Prati to the north only resulted in the removal of the section of walls built by Paul IV around Borgo Pio. But in the 1930s the opening of Via della Conciliazione completely upset the most ancient part of the area, half destroying the *Città Leonina*.

During our walk we'll go through the old and new streets, pointing out the remaining signs of the past splendor of the city of the popes, and discovering the hidden charm of this neighborhood—destination of millions of tourists and pilgrims, but rarely explored beyond its two major monuments, St. Peter's Basilica and Castel Sant'Angelo.

• • • • • • • • • • • • • • • • •

The Vatican

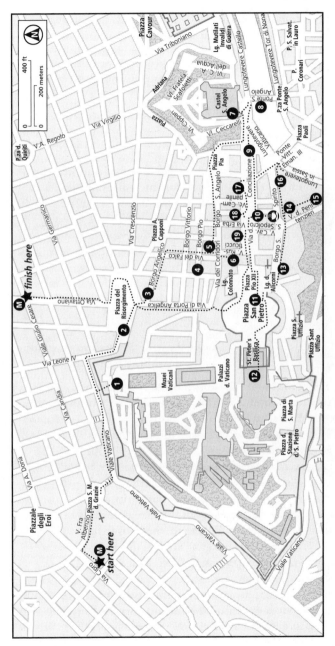

From the Metro stop Cipro take the exit for the Musei Vaticani. Follow Via Fra Albenzio to Piazza Santa Maria delle Grazie and turn right on Via Pisani, descending the ramp of steps to reach Viale Vaticano. In front of you are the ramparts of the walls first built by Leone IV in the 9th century and several times restored. Turn left and follow the walls. To your right opens the entrance to the:

1. **Vatican Museums.** These enormous museums house what is probably the richest art collection in the world; it ranges from ancient Egyptian to Roman and Greek antiquity to Renaissance and baroque, while additional attractions are the fresco decorations of the building itself. Indeed, through the museums you'll have access to the papal apartments—including the Raphael Rooms—and of course the Sistine Chapel, decorated by Michelangelo. Consider 3 hours as a bare minimum for a visit. They are open from mid-March to October, Monday through Friday 8:45am to 4:45pm; and the rest of the year Monday through Saturday from 8:45am to 1:45pm. Admission is charged.

   Bear right following the walls (along a street appropriately called Viale Bastioni di Michelangelo) to:

2. **Piazza del Risorgimento.** This square was created at the end of the 19th century when the neighborhood of Prati—extending all the way north and west—was developed. On the square and to your right is the only surviving section of the walls built by Pius IV, the remainder of which were destroyed in the 19th century. You can still see a few salvaged fragments of the elegant gate—Porta Angelica—that led into the pope's city, including the decorative carving of angels that gave their name to the gate. The gate had a less exalted aspect as well: On the Porta Angelica were hung the heads of those who had been executed, displayed inside a special cage.

   Turn right into Via di Porta Angelica, entering Borgo Pio. The present aspect of this street dates from the 1940s, when it was enlarged by taking down all the buildings on its eastern side (and on the western side of the parallel Via del Mascherino) and replacing them with modern constructions. Turn left onto:

3. **Borgo Angelico.** This was the street at the edge of the walls of Borgo Pio, which run its whole length down to Castel Sant'Angelo (see stop 7).

   Turn right in Via del Falco and cross Borgo Vittorio. This is named not for one of Italy's new kings, as are so many other streets and monuments in Rome, but for the victory at Lepanto over the Turks in 1571. Continue on Via del Falco to:

4. **Borgo Pio.** This is the best preserved of the streets of the Borgo, showing the typical characteristics of the neighborhood, with small houses and traditional craft shops. Here and there you will notice later additions, such as the house at number 18, right at the corner with Via del Falco—an elegant 18th-century building in the style of Borromini—and the building at number 51, in Liberty (Art Nouveau) style from 1909.

   Continue on Via del Falco to Via dei Corridori. This is named for the:

5. **Passetto** (also called *Corridoio*), the not-so-secret passage built by Pope Nicholas III in the 13th century between the Vatican Palace and Castel Sant'Angelo. This elevated corridor was used for safety purposes by the popes, so that they could rapidly take refuge in the nearby fortress in case of attack. The opening in the walls—these were the original walls built by Leo IV in the 9th century—were added by Pius IV to connect Borgo Pio to the *Città Leonina.* As you walk along the street, notice the carvings bearing the arms of the various popes who had the passage restored.

   Also along Via dei Corridori, some of the buildings taken down during the construction of Via della Conciliazione were rebuilt, saving at least some of the ancient neighborhood. Turn right onto Via Rusticucci and proceed to number 14 of Via Rusticucci; there, off to your right, is the facade of:

6. **Palazzo Jacopo da Brescia.** This elegant building is named after the physician of Pope Leo X who had it built, and originally faced on Borgo Nuovo (see Via della Conciliazione, later). It was designed and built by Raphael before 1520.

Retrace your steps and turn right onto Via dei Corridori. Further along at number 44 is the house of another doctor—Febo Brigotti, physician of Pope Paul III—which has also been moved from its original location on Borgo Nuovo. Continue on Borgo Sant'Angelo, which once had houses attached to the walls (demolished in 1938), following the Passetto as it connects to:

7. **Castel Sant'Angelo (also Hadrian's Mausoleum).**
This was originally the emperor Hadrian's monumental tomb. He began building it in A.D. 123 and is buried here, together with all the members of his family down to emperor Caracalla, who was killed in 217. The emperor Aurelian transformed the mausoleum into a fortress in 271 as he was building a new set of city walls. The fortress became the city's main defensive post, and if it didn't help the Romans defend themselves from the Goths, it did help the Goths (once they had taken over the city) keep the Byzantines at bay. When the popes returned to Rome in the 14th century, they immediately started a series of works to strengthen the fortress and transform it into a forbidding castle. The interior was richly decorated for the pope's apartments, while the basement was used as a prison. The fortification was somewhat maimed at the end of the 19th century, when it was separated by the bridge over the Tiber (see below) during construction of the new embankment and road (the Lungotevere). The fortification suffered again in 1934, when it was "isolated," according to the prevailing model of the day, and surrounded by gardens.

The bronze statue of the Archangel Michael on top of the castle dates from the 18th century and replaces a 16th century marble of the same subject (which now resides inside the castle). The statue celebrates a miraculous vision of Pope Gregory the Great. Back in the 6th century A.D., Rome was suffering a terrible plague, so the pope organized a great procession from the Basilica of San Giovanni in Laterano to St. Peter's to beg for forgiveness and the lifting of the plague. At the end of the procession he had a vision of a resplendent angel resheathing his sword right atop Hadrian's Mausoleum. Beside the statue is the *Campana della Misericordia* (bell of mercy), used to announce capital executions. The castle can be visited Tuesday through Sunday from 9am to 8pm. Admission is charged.

In front of the castle's main entrance is:

8. **Ponte Sant'Angelo.** This is Rome's most scenic bridge and a wonderful masterpiece of baroque decoration. The three central arches of the bridge are from the original *Pons Aelius* built by Emperor Hadrian in A.D. 133 to connect his mausoleum with the city. The two remaining arches, one at each end, were rebuilt in the 19th century to connect the bridge with the new streets and embankments. Pope Clement VII started the redecoration project in 1534 by adding statues of St. Paul and St. Peter on the side across the river from Castel Sant'Angelo. Pope Clement IX asked Giovanni Lorenzo Bernini to complete the project, which he did in his usual masterly way, designing 10 angels carrying the symbols of the Passion of Christ. Then he had them carved by his best students and assistants under his supervision. The bridge is truly a sculpture garden as well as a thoroughfare. It is also a marketplace where you will find wall-to-wall trinket sellers hawking wind-up toys and calabashes, and thick crowds of tourists at peak times (keep an eye on your purse or wallet!).

Turn right left along the river and proceed straight into:

9. **Via della Conciliazione.** As with other urban projects executed in Rome under the Fascist regime, the opening of this road has been much criticized—although never as much as the destructive Imperial Fori (see Walking Tour 1)—because the demolitions got a bit out of hand and more was taken down than was necessary. This monumental approach to St. Peter's was obtained in 1932 by demolishing the line of buildings between the two parallel streets that connected the basilica with the Tiber: Borgo Vecchio and Borgo Nuovo. Borgo Vecchio was a long portico—the *Portica*—which followed the ancient Roman Via Cornelia and was the original pilgrimage road to St. Peter's tomb. The Borgo Nuovo—initially called Borgo Alessandrino in honor of Pope Alexander VI who

ordered it—was built for the Jubilee of 1500 and was lined with elegant palaces of cardinals and other important families. Apparently, too many buildings were demolished—including some on the outer perimeter of the street—and the monumental lampposts that now line the avenue were designed and strategically placed in 1950 to hide the irregularity.

The two first buildings on either side were built in the 1940s to replace the ones torn down. Across the street at number 33 is the:

10. **Palazzo dei Penitenzieri,** still standing in its original position. This 15th-century palace now houses a hotel as well as the seat of the Knights of the Holy Sepulcher of Jerusalem. Its two wings—richly frescoed—surround a large central courtyard with terraced garden, which from spring to early autumn houses the hotel's restaurant.

🍵 **Take a Break**   You can have lunch or dinner at **La Veranda,** the restaurant of the hotel inside the 15th-century Palazzo dei Penitenzieri, across the street. The menu always includes some Renaissance items besides other gourmet choices. In the summer, tables are also set in the courtyard garden. You can enter from the hotel in Via della Conciliazione, or from the courtyard entrance at Borgo Santo Spirito 73.

Next, at number 51, is the 16th century **Palazzo Cesi,** while across the street at number 44 is the rebuilt **Palazzo Rusticucci,** which used to be in the square at the end of Borgo Nuovo and Borgo Vecchio. Past those you'll find yourself on Piazza Pio XII, and in front of you opens the spectacular:

11. **Piazza San Pietro,** masterpiece of Bernini, with its majestic colonnade and the huge obelisk at its center. The obelisk graced the Forum of Alexandria in Egypt until A.D. 37, when Caligula had it brought over to decorate his circus (which was later finished by Nero). While the circus disappeared, the obelisk remained standing on the side of the basilica until 1586, when Pope Sixtus V had it moved to its present location. Cross the square to a circular stone on the pavement; from that spot slowly spin in a

circle and notice how the colonnade seems to be made of one single row of columns.

Closing the scenic colonnade is:

12. **St. Peter's Basilica.** The first basilica was built by emperor Constantine and consecrated in A.D. 326. In the 15th century, it was decided to build a new, more grandiose basilica over the old one, as a symbol of the increasing power of the Roman Catholic Church and its claim as the direct heir of Jesus' ministry. The new church was consecrated in 1626, 1,300 years after the first one (and in the thick of the Reformation).

The church is chock-full of works of art and both architectural and archaeological wonders—you can visit the grottoes under the church, where excavations have identified burials going back to the time of St. Peter. Among the most famous works of art in St. Peter's is the *Pietà* by Michelangelo, a statue of transcendent beauty carved by the artist at the age of 24. The main altar, the Altar of the Confession, sits in the middle of the basilica and is carved from a single block of marble. The monumental bronze baldachin (canopy) that rises above the altar was designed by Bernini. This has an interesting— and gossipy—story. Pope Urban VIII commissioned Bernini to create the work, allegedly in thanks to God for saving the life of a young woman very dear to him, and the child she was carrying. Take a moment to examine the marble pedestals that support the four columns of the *baldacchino*. Notice the weird carvings that surround the pope's coat of arms carved on these pedestals (they read right to left). Naughty Bernini has printed in stone the memory of the episode, carving a diminutive woman's face above and a female reproductive organ below in the different stages of delivery, from rest, to labor, to birth.

This is not the only story about Urban VIII and the *baldacchino*. One of the most famous *Pasquinate*—short notes criticizing the government that were secretly appended to the "talking" statue of Pasquino (see Walking Tour 2) during the night—stated "What the Barbarians did not do, the Barberini did," playing on the alliteration between *Barbari* (Barbarians) and *Barberini* (the pope's family name). The criticism refers to the fact that the pope obtained the bronze for the *baldacchino* by removing it from the Pantheon's porch ceiling (see Walking Tour 3). He used the remainder of his ill-gotten bronze to cast 80 cannons for Castel Sant'Angelo that shot salvos of blanks during the Jubilee celebrations in 1625. The Romans felt it was a rather vainglorious reason to maim a monument that had stood for 1,600 years.

Walking back through Piazza San Pietro, exit the colonnade to your right and take **Borgo Santo Spirito.** This street was the heart of the Saxon pilgrims' settlement by Saint Peter's. You'll see immediately to your right the church:

13. **Santi Michele e Magno,** which you can enter by climbing the steep staircase at number 21. This church dates to the 9th century and was the religious center for the settlement of Frisians in Rome. Although redone in the 12th and then again in the 18th century, you can still see the antique columns supporting the naves; the cosmatesque floor is also original.

     Continue on, passing to your left the apse of another medieval church, San Lorenzo in Piscibus, enclosed in a courtyard. Turn right on Via dei Penitenzieri, where you'll find to your left the portals of:

14. **Santo Spirito in Sassia.** Redone several times—last in the 16th century, according to a design by Antonio da Sangallo il Giovane—over the original 8th-century church, this was the headquarters of the Saxon pilgrims and was originally named Santa Maria in Sassia. The interior is in typical Renaissance style and decorated with 16th-century frescoes.

     Further on, Via dei Penitenzieri ends in the arch of:

15. **Porta Santo Spirito.** This powerful and elegant gate in the Vatican walls was designed by Sangallo il Giovane, who started building it in 1543. Michelangelo was in charge of the overall project for the Vatican fortifications and wasn't the easiest-going of geniuses. Whatever the reason—fit of temper or otherwise—the two architects had a serious disagreement on the fortification design and work had to be interrupted; the gate was never finished.

Retrace your steps and turn right on Borgo Santo Spirito again. At number 2 of Borgo Santo Spirito is the arch of 1664—by the ever-present Giovanni Lorenzo Bernini—giving entrance to the:

16. **Hospital of Santo Spirito in Sassia.** Enlarged in the 15th and 16th centuries and partially redone in the 20th, it was established in the 12th century by Pope Innocent III over the almost abandoned Saxon settlement (hence the name "in Sassia"). It was run by the religious order of the Santo Spirito according to the oldest known set of hospital regulations, the *Liber Regulae,* and was financially independent.

Outside the Bernini arch to the left, notice the *ruota degli esposti,* the contraption where newborns were abandoned for adoption, and the box for the donations. A sort of combination Lazy Susan and night-deposit box, parents would put the baby in and turn the "wheel" *(ruota),* which brought the orphan inside the hospital. Just inside of the arch is the beautifully decorated 15th-century portal that gave access to the hospital.

The hospital is still in operation today (the "wheel" is not), and you can access it from its main entrance on Via di Lungotevere in Sassia 1, facing the Tiber. Inside, behind the facade redone in the 20th century, you can still see the elegant courtyards and have a glimpse of the 15th-century frescoed ceilings of the *Corsia Sistina.* The hospital houses the interesting **National Historical Museum of Sanitary Art,** which exhibits anatomic tables and models as well as a collection of Roman and Arab surgical instruments.

Turn left out of the hospital and take Via San Pio X to your left; cross Via della Conciliazione and walk down its right-hand side; to your right is the church of:

17. **Santa Maria in Traspontina,** rebuilt here in the 16th century after the original near Castel Sant'Angelo was demolished to make room for the new set of fortifications. Particular care was taken to make the cupola sit low so that it wouldn't interfere with the line of fire of Castel Sant'Angelo's cannons. The interior is decorated with frescoes—among which are some by the Cavalier d'Arpino—while on the baroque main altar is an icon of the Virgin Mary brought back from Jerusalem by Carmelite friars in

the 12th century. A special relic is preserved in the third chapel to the left; here, by the altar, lie two columns, which are said to be the very ones to which the apostles Peter and Paul were attached to be flagellated.

Turn right onto Vicolo del Campanile, to the left of the church, where you can see the **church's bell tower** from the 17th century and the **facade of a house** decorated with *bugnato* (decorative wall art) around its portal and faded graffiti by either Virgilio Romano or Polidoro da Caravaggio from 1520.

Back on Via della Conciliazione, at number 15 is the facade of the 16th century **Palace of the Prisons,** rebuilt here from its original location across from the church of Santa Maria in Traspontina. Further on, at number 30, is the elegant:

18. **Palazzo Torlonia,** one of the few remaining original buildings of the area. It bears the name of the Torlonia, a family of Roman princes, who bought it in 1820 and added another wing in the back. It was originally built in 1500 for Cardinal Adriano Castellesi and then donated to Henry the VIII of England, who used it as residence for his ambassador.

Further along on Via della Conciliazione at numbers 32, 34, and 36 is the:

19. **Palazzo della Congregazione per le Chese Orientali,** a rebuild of the Palazzo dei Convertendi, which originally stood across from Palazzo Torlonia (above). The original palace was built in the 16th century and integrated the preexisting Palazzo Caprini, which was designed by Bramante and was also the location of Raphael's death in 1520.

Follow to the right the Colonnade of Piazza San Pietro—here is the Post Office of the Vatican, where you can mail some postcards with fancy stamps—and pass under the *Passetto*. Turn right onto Via di Porta Angelica. Continue on to Piazza Risorgimento, and cross the square to **Via Ottaviano,** a good shopping street, where you can make some purchases on your way back to the Ottaviano subway station on the corner of Viale Giulio Cesare.

Aventino

Start: Metro stop Circo Massimo.

Finish: Metro stop Circo Massimo.

Time: 2½ hours, excluding time for visits.

Best Time: Morning Monday through Saturday and late afternoon Tuesday through Saturday.

Worst Time: Sundays and the lunch lull when churches are closed to visits; also Monday afternoon if you want to visit Caracalla Baths.

T he Aventine Hill (*Aventino* in Italian) was given to the people of Rome by the *lex Icilia* in 456 B.C. for plebeian residences. However, under Augustus at the beginning of the 1st century the hill began to be occupied by elegant patrician homes. By the end of the Roman Empire, the formerly working-class district was covered with luxurious dwellings—which is why the barbarian invaders, in particular the Visigoth Alaric, caused especially fierce destruction here.

By the Middle Ages, when the population of Rome had dwindled and shrunk away from the hills to concentrate near the Tiber, the Aventine had been almost completely reclaimed by vegetation, with only a few monasteries and fortified dwellings interspersed between fields and vineyards. During the 16th century, the fields were transformed into elegant gardens and villas, and a few religious buildings were constructed. Thereafter, the neighborhood remained basically untouched until the 20th century, when a few elegant town houses and small villas were built on its slopes. A few decades after, in 1931, the whole area was developed, causing a great loss of archaeological remains. For the most part, only the names of these older structures survive today, preserved in the streets and squares built over them.

The Aventine maintains its own strong attraction and is a surprising island of silence in the heart of Rome. On the main hill of the Aventine you will step back a few centuries as you wander among medieval churches and monasteries, gardens, and picturesque views. On San Saba—the Little Aventine—you'll find yourself in an exclusive residential neighborhood of great charm.

• • • • • • • • • • • • • • • • •

Exit from the metro station of Circo Massimo; the large modern building immediately behind you is the seat of FAO, the United Nations Food and Agriculture Organization. Turn right onto Viale delle Terme di Caracalla. This avenue was designed in the 19th century as part of the "archeological Promenade" stretching from Piazza Venezia to Via Appia Antica; the Promenade was meant to protect the monuments from developers, but ironically, in 1940 its green alleys were turned into motorways to connect with the current main artery, Via Cristoforo Colombo. You can still enjoy the massive trees shading the broad sidewalks, though. A little farther along to your right, past a small stadium built in 1939, you'll find the entrance to the:

1. **Terme di Caracalla.** These thermal baths, built by Emperor Caracalla in A.D. 212, were a grandiose feat of architecture and engineering, and could accommodate up to 1,600 customers at the same time. The cisterns contained 80,000 liters (over 20,000 gal.) of water, and beneath the complex there was what amounted to a small town that worked to keep the baths going. Its network of

Aventino

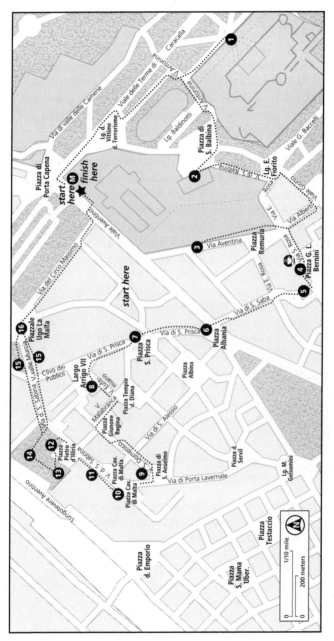

subterranean streets and corridors was used for carts to bring loads of wood for the furnaces and supplies of fresh towels for the bathers. The baths were much more than a spa; they also included a gym with both indoor and outdoor facilities, exercise rooms, a stadium, and a library with several reading rooms and meeting rooms. There were also places to unwind: covered porticoes to stroll and small gardens to rest in.

The whole complex was richly decorated with marble, mosaics, stuccowork, and frescoes. The baths were a service provided by the government to the population—the plebeians, that is, since the rich patricians had their own private facilities at home. Caracalla's baths remained in use until A.D. 537, when the Goths cut the aqueduct and stopped the water supply. The ruins—with walls still soaring to great heights—are impressive, and a guided tour best recreates the past grandeur for the visitor. Few of the original decorations are still visible, because the baths were excavated in the 16th century and much was moved to private and public collections. Some of the greatest ancient Roman works of art have come from here, including the famous mosaic with athletes (now at the Vatican Museums, see Walking Tour 8), and the so-called Farnese bull and Hercules (now at the Museo Archeologico Nazionale in Naples). It is open Tuesday through Sunday from 9am to 1 hour before sunset and Mondays from 9am to 2pm.

Retrace your steps and turn left into Via Antonina, skirting the ruins of the Caracalla Baths to Piazza di Santa Balbina. Here is the church of:

2. **Santa Balbina.** This is one of Rome's most ancient churches, dating back to the 5th or 6th century A.D. It has been restored many times through the centuries. In the 12th century the mosaic decorations in the apse fell off and were later replaced with frescoes. In 1927 the baroque decorations (and many from later ages, as well) were removed, giving the church its current look. The floor mosaics were added in 1939, brought here from the necropolis excavated during the construction of the Via

dei Fori Imperiali nearby. Inside you can still see the 16th-century frescoes in the apse and some of the earlier frescoes (13th and 14th c.) in the chapels.

Continue on Via di Santa Balbina past Largo Fioritto into the pleasant Viale Giotto, which is shaded by trees. A short distance away, Viale Giotto approaches the Aurelian city walls, built in the 3rd century A.D. Before reaching the walls, turn right in Via Alberti, and follow it to Piazza Remuria. You can stroll beyond the square to:

3. **Via Aventina** where, if you are interested in modern architecture, you can admire some excellent examples of the rationalistic and modernist style from the 1930s.

Retrace your steps across Piazza Remuria and turn right into Via Salvatore Rosa where you can:

Take a Break If you would like to stop for lunch (or dinner, as the case may be), **Al Callarello,** Via Salvator Rosa 8 (© **06/5747575**), is a wonderful restaurant specializing in seafood, including such rarities as *carpaccio di polpo* (thinly sliced, cured octopus served with herbs), as well as standards like *spaghetti alle vongole* (spaghetti with clams). In good weather you can sit outside, too.

Continue down Via Salvatore Rosa, which soon opens onto Piazza G.L. Bernini, the heart of the:

4. **Complex of the Instituto Case Popolari San Saba.** This complex of popular housing is the first development built on this hill after ancient Roman times. The houses, raised between 1907 and 1923, take the whole slope of the hill between Piazza Bernini and Viale Giotto. The small and pleasant brick buildings decorated with stucco and travertine marble will probably make this the most beautiful housing project you will ever stroll through.

Cross over Piazza Bernini to Via di San Saba where, immediately to your right, is the church of:

5. **San Saba,** giving its name to the whole neighborhood and housing the remains of Saba, the abbot from Palestine who started the monastic movement that swept Europe

throughout the Middle Ages and beyond. His body was brought here by his followers after his death and buried in the church they founded in the 7th century A.D. You can access the church from the courtyard of the attached convent. Legend has it that this church was built over the oratory of Saint Silvia, the mother of Pope Gregory the Great. The Latin inscription over the portal *(Ex qua domo cotidie pia mater mittebat ad clivum Scauri scutellam leguminum)* states that the pious mother exited this house every day to bring a bowl of soup to an address in Clivio Scauro, and indeed Gregory lived in the monastery of Sant'Andrea on that street.

In 768, the antipope Constantine II was imprisoned here after having been blinded in punishment. Inside are frescoes of the 12th and 13th centuries; particularly well preserved are the ones in the nave to the left, which include a painting of three naked women—a little surprising in a church—which refers to the miracle of San Nicola di Bari (St. Nicholas of Bari) and the three spinsters. The story goes that they were the three very beautiful daughters of a very poor father who was frantic with worry because he had no money for their dowry, and worried that their beauty exposed them to great risk (of losing their virtue). He invoked St. Nicholas in deep despair, and the saint threw a large bag full of gold through the girls' bedroom window, which allowed them to marry.

Continue down Via di San Saba to:

6. **Piazza Albania.** This square is built in the small valley that divides the two areas of the Aventine Hill, over a gate in the Servian walls; built in the 6th century B.C., these were Rome's first city walls. The walls were abandoned when the next set of walls were built farther out, but you can still see two sections of the Servian walls at the corner of Via Sant'Anselmo to the southwest of the square. From the gate started *Vicus Piscinae Publicae* (Public Pool Street), which is today's Viale Aventino descending to your right. The *Vicus* was named after the large pool created nearby to collect the waters from the local springs and provide bathing for the people before the Baths of Caracalla were built. Of the various springs, one was dedicated to

Mercury and was used by merchants who needed to purify themselves after illicit trades; another was under the protection of Apollo and had healing properties for the spleen.

Cross Piazza Albania and take Via di Santa Prisca, climbing towards the right. At the end of this street is Piazza Santa Prisca where, to your right, you'll see the church of:

7. **Santa Prisca.** Even older than Santa Balbina (see stop 2), this church started as a small oratory in the 3rd century A.D., which was then enlarged into a church in the 5th century. It was restored in the 8th century from which date the decorations under the arches of the sacristy and the cornice of the apse, still visible. The church was shortened in the 15th century because the first three arches collapsed, and given a new facade in the 17th century. Under the church (access is from a door at the very beginning of the right nave) are the crypt and the **Mitreo of Santa Prisca,** an archaeological area excavated from 1934 and 1966 that includes a house from the 1st century A.D. and a temple to the god Mitra, with well-preserved frescoes depicting the initiation ceremonies.

Cross the square and continue on Via di Santa Prisca to:

8. **Largo Arrigo VII,** which contains the only visible Roman ruins surviving from the development of this area of the hill in the 1930s. Three rooms decorated with frescoes and stucco open onto a portico; they belong to a Roman home from the 1st century B.C.

Take Via Eufemiano to Piazza Tempio di Diana, named for the Temple of Diana that stood nearby; turn right on Via Malabranca and cross Piazza Giunone Regina (named for another lost Roman temple) to turn left onto Via San Domenico. At the end of this street, cross Piazza di Sant'Anselmo and turn right into Via di Porta Lavernale. Here, to your right is the alley giving access to the church and monastery of:

9. **Sant'Anselmo.** The church is from the 19th century, but inside the convent you can still admire some beautiful

mosaics from the 2nd and 3rd centuries A.D. that originally belonged to the Roman house over which the monastery was built.

Continue on Via di Porta Lavernale, which opens to your left into Piazza Cavalieri di Malta. Here is the majestic:

10. **Complesso dell'Ordine dei Cavalieri di Malta.** Started in 939 as a Benedictine convent, it was taken over by the Knights Templar in the 12th century and the Gerosolimitani friars in the 14th. The monastery and gardens are surrounded by a high wall decorated with symbols from the coat of arms of Cardinal Rezzonico, who had the complex reorganized and the church inside built in the 18th century. Walk to the portal at number 3 and look through the round hole you'll find there; it frames a perfect view of St. Peter's cupola.

Turn right on Via di Santa Sabina, passing at number 2 the entrance to the Convent of Sant'Alessio, rebuilt in the 18th century over the original monastery from the 10th century, to the church of:

11. **San Bonifacio e Sant'Alessio.** This church was built in the 8th century over a previous one dedicated to San Bonifacio and was then redone in the 12th century, and again in the 18th century when some of the mosaic floors were destroyed. At number 23 you can enter a portico—notice to your right the fragment of a Gothic spire with the carvings of St. Bonifacio and St. Alessio—retracing the original medieval courtyard that gives access to the church. Across the courtyard is the 18th-century facade of the church and, to the right, the elegant bell tower from the 13th century, with five orders of arched windows. You can access the church by passing under the cosmatesque portal. Inside, under the apse is the only Romanesque crypt in Rome; it is decorated with 12th-century frescoes. The main altar houses the remains of St. Thomas of Canterbury, while the column is thought to be the one where St. Sebastian was chained during his martyrdom.

Continue along Via di Santa Sabina, where a bit farther along, you'll reach the church of:

12. **Santa Sabina,** the best extant example of a Christian basilica from the 5th century. Founded in 425 by Pietro d'Illiria, it was further decorated in the following centuries. In the 13th century the cloister and the bell tower were built (the tower was shortened in the 17th c.). Restored in the 15th century, its interior was redone by Domenico Fontana and Francesco Borromini between the 16th and 17th centuries, but these additions were completely taken down by two successive restorations in the 20th century. The basilica contains a few spectacular treasures, such as the carved wooden portals from the 5th century, and has an atmospheric, luminous interior. The annexed convent was founded by St. Domenico and had among its teachers St. Thomas Aquinas; rebuilt in the 20th century, only a few parts are still original.

The lateral portico of the church gives a prospect onto:

13. **Piazza Pietro d'Illiria.** This square did not exist until 1614, when it was opened by breaking into the medieval fortress, of which you can still see the walls. Built by Alberico II in the 10th century, it passed to the Savelli in the 11th century, and later to the Dominican friars. The fountain to the right is by Giacomo della Porta, with a granite tub taken from thermal baths nearby.

The rest of the fortress was transformed in 1932 into the:

14. **Parco Savello,** commonly called the Giardino degli Aranci (Orange Garden). This pleasant garden surrounded by medieval walls is considered one of the loveliest in Rome and affords great views over St. Peter's.

Continue down Via di Santa Sabina and cross Clivo dei Publicii, Rome's first paved road, laid in 289 B.C. Beyond is Via di Valle Murcia where, at numbers 6 and 7, is the:

15. **Roseto Municipale (Municipal Rose Garden).** This is a magical garden with about 5,000 rose bushes of over 1,000 varieties. Among these are some extremely rare specimens, admired by experts around the world. The rose garden reserves part of its grounds for the cultivation

of plants participating in the International Rose Show, a competition for new varieties of roses. The display, held in May and June when the roses bloom, is spectacular.

The street ends in:

16. **Piazzale Ugo La Malfa,** a large square graced by a statue of Giuseppe Mazzini, the great Italian republican leader, put here in 1949 for the centenary of the short-lived Roman Republic. From the square you can enjoy a unique view over the ruins of the Palatine Hill (see Walking Tour 1).

Turn right on Via del Circo Massimo, which follows the perimeter of the Roman Circus (see Walking Tour 1) back to the subway stop under the FAO building.

Villa Borghese

Start: Entrance to Villa Borghese off Via Pinciana. Bus 52, 53, and 910 all stop in Via Pinciana by the entrance, while the electric bus 116 leaves you inside, right in front of the Casino Nobile.

Finish: Porta Pinciana, Metro stop Spagna or bus 490 to Piazza del Popolo.

Time: 2½ hours excluding museum visits and other activities.

Best Time: Daytime Tuesday through Sunday when the museums are open.

Worst Time: Nighttime and Monday when the museums are closed.

At the heart of modern Rome is a park beloved by locals and discovered with astonishment by the lucky—or well-informed—visitor. Many people visit a gallery or two on the edges of the park, and venture no further. That so much greenery (acres and acres of it) could exist only a few steps from the busy Via del Corso and Piazza di Spagna seems unthinkable, and yet you can still find peace and beauty in Villa Borghese as you could over 4 centuries ago. With five museums and grounds richly landscaped and decorated with works of art, this is much more than a stroll through

143

the shrubbery—it is a walk through a slice of Roman culture with roots in the ancient past.

The history of the villa as it is today dates from 1580, when the Borghese family acquired a modest vineyard on the hill behind the Pincio. At that time, some of the rich and noble families in Rome had started building suburban retreats to escape the noise and stress of city life, following a pattern established by their ancient predecessors back in the 2nd and 3rd centuries B.C. The Borghese were on a rapid political and social path of ascension: The family went from being rich Sienese merchants to princes of the realm—and even a Borghese pope—in one generation.

The father, Marcantonio, emigrated from Siena in the 16th century to be nearer the church and the seat of its power; so well did he succeed that his son, Camillo Borghese, was elected pope in 1605. As Pope Paul V, Camillo immediately started helping his family's quest for advancement (in which they excelled), acquiring a title of nobility. He gave particular support to his nephew Scipione, who had become a cardinal. At the beginning of the 17th century, Cardinale Scipione started ed acquiring land around the family vineyard with the purpose of turning it into a *villa delle delizie* (villa of delights) that would surpass in beauty all the other elegant country retreats in Rome and be a symbol of the family's social status. And because this ambitious family had also been busily collecting works of art, both ancient and modern, the villa was meant to house a private museum as well.

Work began in 1606, which was to transform the vineyards into a marvel of art and nature by its completion in 1616. Following the classic tradition, the villa included a *pars urbana* (urban part) consisting of a group of elegant buildings called the *casini* (lodges or pavilions); these pavilions were surrounded by formal gardens elaborately decorated with fountains and statues. The villa also included a *pars rustica* (rustic part), where nature was left to itself with little landscaping. The formal gardens consisted of the *giardino boschereccio* surrounding the Casino Nobile (today the Gallerie Borghese), and the Parco dei Daini (the prince's private ground); these two gardens were divided by the totally enclosed **Giardini Segreti** (Secret Gardens, later in this chapter). The buildings, including the Casino Nobile, were meant for recreational purposes and not for habitation; the family residential palace was

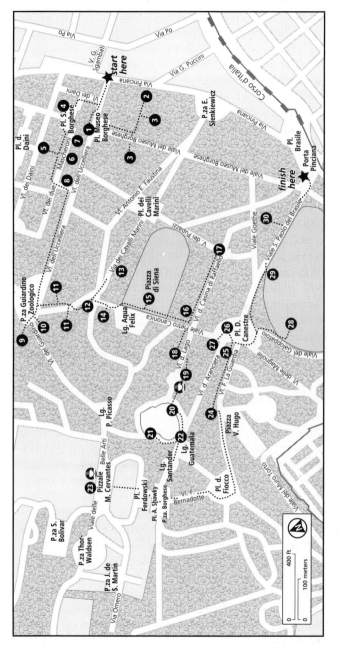

in the city (see Walking Tour 4). The third section of the villa—the "rustic" grounds—were left wild and used as a hunting preserve. Antiquities were used to decorate the park and the Casino Nobile, where Scipione moved his art collection (more artwork decorated the family palace in town).

At the end of the 18th century, Marcantonio IV Borghese decided to renovate and embellish the park; this is when the **Giardino del Lago** (see stop 20) was created, following the English garden style then in vogue. At the beginning of the 19th century the family bought three other smaller villas on the adjoining Pincio and asked the architect Luigi Canina to redesign the grounds to the south of the villa. He opened the new entrance by Porta del Popolo (off Piazza del Popolo).

In 1901, after over 10 years of legal negotiations, the villa was acquired by the Italian government and then passed on to the municipality of Rome. When the creator of the villa—Cardinal Scipione—died in 1633, he stated in his will that his heirs were to keep the tradition of hospitality of the villa, opening it to the public. It was indeed a long-established tradition that on certain occasions the park was opened for people to come and stroll in the alleys of trees and graveled paths. An inscription on the walls of the villa—the marble plaque was stolen around 1750—declared the opening of the villa to the public on Thursdays and Sundays. Romans were not the only ones who availed themselves of the opportunity; already in Goethe's time, visitors to the Eternal City found relief from the heavy labor of visiting churches and ruins in the quiet of the park. Scipione's will gave leverage for the acquisition of the villa by the government, successfully stopping the attempt at developing the grounds for residential purposes.

The gallery opened to the public in 1902, while the gardens opened more than a year later due to further legal squabbles. The government renamed the park Villa Umberto I (after the king who had been assassinated 2 years before), but the new name did not stick, and people kept referring to it as Villa Borghese. Foreign governments then started donating statues and busts commemorating poets who had loved and spent time in the villa. Leading the way was German Emperor William II, who in 1903 donated a statue of Goethe to commemorate the poet in the villa he loved. These gifts were the origin of the park's "alley of poets," with busts of Russian

Pushkin, Persian Ferdousi, and Egyptian Shawky among others (see Via Bernadotte, stop 23).

In later years the grounds were nearly abandoned, many of its alleys were paved, and cars allowed inside. The deterioration didn't prevent Romans from flowing in on weekends with their families, but the government finally found the funds for a major restoration project that slowly brought back the villa to its 16th-century splendor. With its 80 hectares (148 acres), Villa Borghese is now one of the largest public parks in Rome—and the only one in the center of the city—and its appeal ranges from art lovers visiting its museums and works of art, people coming for its quiet paths or the views, lovers and families enjoying picnics, skaters, bikers, joggers, and theater lovers.

• • • • • • • • • • • • • • • • •

A note: You can rent bicycles—and a variety of other wheeled pedal-powered contraptions—at various points along the park. Hence the whole "walk" could become a ride—maybe in one of the four-seat buggies—if you so chose. It is common practice to leave a picture ID for security with the bike rental agent, so make sure you have something else besides your passport (which you might want to keep in the safe at your hotel), such as your driver's license (but not your Elks membership card—it has to be a government-issued ID).

Start at the entrance of the villa off Via Pinciana (corner Via G. Sgambati). Opening in front of you is the:

1. **Casino Nobile (Pavilion of the Nobility).** This is the park's main building, built between 1606 and 1616 following a design by Flaminio Ponzio and Jan Van Santen—the Dutch architect known by his Italianized name of Giovanni Vasanzio. Today, as back then, the pavilion houses the rich art collection of Cardinale Scipione Borghese, but between its first opening to the public in 1902 and its grand reopening in 1997 it suffered a few decades of abandonment and neglect; when cars were allowed within the park, the building was surrounded by a parking lot. The lengthy restoration brought the villa back to its original 17th-century beauty, including the elegant balustrade around the courtyard. Some things could not be restored; at the time of Cardinale Scipione,

the art display began outside the building, whose facade and sides were richly decorated with antique sculptures and reliefs (as was the balustrade). Unfortunately, all the ancient Roman artwork—including what was inside Cardinale Scipione's collection—was removed in 1807 by Napoleon and is now in the Louvre in Paris. The balustrade is a copy of the 17th-century original, from 1895.

So you'll have to content yourself with the collection inside the museum—which remains one of the most amazing assemblages of masterpieces anywhere. You will find the **Museo Borghese** on the first floor, and the **Galleria Borghese** on the second. They are considered the finest private collection in the world and one of the most important collections of art in Europe. The acquisition of the collection was done with the Borghese family's typical determination and skill. For example, when Pope Paul V came to power, one of his jobs was the completion of the new St. Peter's Basilica; having had the old facade torn down, he found himself with a lot of surplus antique statues and carvings. These pieces, which had decorated the old facade, he swiftly passed to his nephew. The family also actively collected artwork by funding excavation campaigns in search of ancient Roman art, and by commissioning works directly from the great artists of the time, which is how Cardinale Scipione became the protector of Giovanni Lorenzo Bernini.

Much of the Borghese art collections miraculously escaped the Napoleonic occupation—or maybe not so miraculously, given that Camillo Borghese, with another display of the family's political acumen (or possibly just luck), had become the second husband of Paolina Bonaparte, Napoleon's little sister. But Camillo did have to relinquish to France his personal collection—the original content of the Museo Borghese—which is now the core of the Louvre's Roman antiquity collection. It was not such a bad deal, since he got to keep some of his garden decorations as well as his Bernini masterpieces and the unique collection of paintings, including Raphael, Caravaggio, Domenichino, Andrea del Sarto, Veronese, and much more. The rich collection of Roman antiquities now on display in the museum comes from the Borghese's city palace (see Walking Tour 4) and other villas of the family, which only proves how large their collection was. The Museo and Galleria are open Tuesday through Sunday from 9am to 7pm and advance reservations are required. Admission is charged. You'll find a cafe and snack bar in the basement.

At the front of the Casino Nobile are the formal gardens, with shaded alleys opening onto spaces decorated with fountains. Take the Viae del Museo Borghese, which begins at the bottom of the pavilion's main staircase, walk beyond the balustrade, and then turn into the first alley on your left. At the end of it you'll find the:

2. **Grotta dei Vini (Wine Grotto).** This rustic tufa building—designed by Flaminio Ponzio and built together with the villa—was indeed used as a wine cellar and is connected by an underground passage to the Casino Nobile. It was also used as a summer banquet room, following the ancient Roman tradition, and its interior is elaborately decorated with frescoes (those on the vaulted ceiling are still visible, and depict the classical gods' table) and stuccowork.

Begin retracing your steps, but turn left down the first alley you reach; this opens onto:

3. **Fontana Oscura.** One of two almost identical fountains opening on each side of Via del Museo Borghese—this fountain has a round basin and the one across has an oval basin—they owe their name to the blissful shade one can enjoy here in summer. Unfortunately the original decoration of antique statues that surrounded the marble seat as well as the tall edge that surrounded the fountain are gone.

Walk down the alley to your right, cross the Via del Museo Borghese, and admire the second fountain. Take the alley to your right, and turn left on Via del Museo Borghese to come back toward the Casino Nobile. Just to the right of the Casino you will discover the private gardens of the Prince, once reserved for his use and personal guests. Behind the Casino Nobile is:

4. **Piazzale Scipione Borghese,** decorated as a garden. When the Casino Nobile was restored in the 1990s, this whole area was occupied—and destroyed—by the worksite; after the works were over, it was decided to replant

the garden as it was in 1915. Flower beds surround the **Fontana di Venere,** built at the beginning of the 20th century to replace the 17th-century Fontana del Narciso that originally decorated the garden. Back then, a ring of antique statues and four giant hermae—attributed to Pietro and Giovanni Lorenzo Bernini, but probably much older Roman works only restored by them—surrounded the fountain, and two gazebos for guests were strategically located on either side of the fountain in the ilex, or holm-oak, wood.

Walk away from the Casino Nobile, turn on Viale dei Daini, and you will find the entrance to:

5. **Parco dei Daini (Park of the Fallow Deer).** Also called the Parco delle Prospettive (Perspective Garden), this garden was reserved for the Prince. Its area is neatly divided by alleys meeting at right angles and is defined by the 13 colossal **Termini** by Pietro and Giovanni Lorenzo Bernini (or again, maybe antiques, just restored by them). Viale dei Daini ends on two scenic perspectives, the **Frontespizio del Dace** on the eastern side, and the facade of the **Teatro** (theater) on the other, decorated with antique reliefs and carvings. The paths lie in the middle of an ilex wood numbering over 600 trees; the area where deer and other animals were once fenced in for hunting has also been reconstructed.

The southern side of the Parco dei Daini is lined with the:

6. **Giardini Segreti (Secret Gardens).** These were the private gardens of the prince, where he cultivated (or had cultivated) rare and exotic plants. Completely enclosed by walls and gates, the gardens have been restored to their 16th-century appearance, including the selection of spec-imens—particularly the citrus fruits, of which there are some unusual varieties. During their history, the gardens have been replanted several times, changing the species according to the fashion of the moment; the "bulb gar-den" with Dutch tulips of the 16th century was replaced with pineapples when those were brought from America; other successive favorites were carnations, lichens, roses, sunflowers, and peppers, and later anemones, narcissi, and hyacinths. During the Second World War the flower

beds were all transformed into vegetable gardens for food production (cabbages and potatoes, mainly).

The gardens are divided into three sections by two fine buildings: the **Casino dell'Uccelliera** (**Pavilion of the Aviary;** see next stop), which is the closest to the Casino Nobile, and the **Casino della Meridiana** (**Pavilion of the Sundial;** see stop 8). The gardens can be visited by guided tour only, and free tours are organized by the city's Environment and Farm Department (*C* **06/770042** or 06/7004573), usually on the hour between 10am and 1pm, and again from 3pm and 6pm.

Walk along Viale dei due Mascheroni—on the north side of the gardens—leaving the Casino Nobile behind you. You will first see the:

7. **Casino dell'Uccelliera (Pavilion of the Aviary),** which was built together with the Casino Nobile and finished in 1619. It is richly decorated with stuccowork and antique relief sculptures on the outside, while the vaulted interior is frescoed to mimic an arbor with birds. The two large cages integrated in the building—their graceful cupolas are made of ironwork and wire—were filled with rare and beautiful birds at the time of the prince in the 17th century. Between the Casino Nobile and the Aviary is the **Old Garden**—the first to be planted—and on the other side is the **Aviary Garden,** also planted in the early 1600s. The Old Garden was also called the Giardino dei Melangoli, from the 16th-century name of the bitter orange, whereas the Aviary garden was the Giardino dei Fiori—cultivated with rare and exotic flowers, starting with Dutch tulips in the early 17th century.

Continuing on Viale dei Mascheroni you will pass to your left:

8. **Casino della Meridiana (Pavilion of the Sundial),** added in 1680 together with the third section of the Giardini Segreti, the **Garden of the Sundial.** The view from the Pavilion of the Sundial toward its enclosed garden mirrors the view from the Pavilion of the Aviary at the other end. The building is decorated with marble, stuccowork, and—of course—a large sundial. The Casino della Meridiana houses the park information and documentation center.

Turn left around the Pavilion of the Sundial and right on Viale dell'Uccelliera. Soon on your right will be the:

9. **Bioparco (Biopark).** This is a fancy name for the city zoo, and a perfect stop if you have children in tow. A very special kind of zoo from the start, it was inaugurated in 1911 and organized according to the revolutionary principles of Karl Hagenbeck, the German zoo expert who advocated the use of natural barriers instead of iron cages to keep animals separated from each other—and from the visitors coming to see them. The result is much more visually attractive than regular zoos and, one hopes, less stressful for the animals as well. After alternating periods of glory and abandonment, the zoo was completely redone in recent times.

The name "biopark" relates to the newer concept of reducing the number of species and focusing on scientific observation and teaching. The park's grounds cover 17 hectares (42 acres) and contain more than 1,000 animals divided, including 72 species of mammals, 92 species of birds, and 54 species of reptiles, as well as some protected species. The park also doubles as a botanical garden for a variety of plants. The entrance is at Viale del Giardino Zoologico 20, and it is open daily from 9:30am to 5pm from the end of October to the end of March, and till 6pm the rest of the year. Admission is charged. Inside you'll also find a restaurant, bar, and picnic areas.

If you really are into animals, you can also visit the **Museo Civico di Zoologia (Civic Zoology Museum)** with a collection of over five million specimens, including a historic collection of the fauna specific to the Roman countryside. One of the most interesting permanent exhibits is Amori Bestiali (Animal Loves). You can enter the museum from the biopark (or from its main entrance at Via Adrovandi 18) Tuesday to Sunday from 9am to 5pm. Admission is charged.

Across from the zoo is the:

10. **Casino del Graziano (Graziano's Pavilion).** This medieval building was purchased by Cardinal Scipione Borghese in 1616 from the jurist Stefano Graziani and was destined to be a hunting lodge. It has been fully

restored, bringing back the elegant frescoes inside from the 16th and 17th century.

The casino sits at the edge of the:

11. **Valle dei Platani (Valley of the Plane Trees),** a piece of Roman countryside that has survived unchanged since the 17th century. Locals refer to it as the "valley of the dogs" because it is so popular with dog owners, who come here to exercise their animals. As you stroll along the alleys, notice the majestic plane trees: The largest and oldest ones were planted by Cardinal Scipione Borghese back in 1615. This is the oldest area of the villa and contains some 400 different species of plants; it is what remains of the rustic section of the park after the redesign in the 18th century.

Stroll along the alley that crosses the Valle dei Platani till you reach a crossroads of larger alleys marked by the:

12. **Tempio di Antonio e Faustina (Temple of Antoninus and Faustina).** This constructed (that is, fake) ruined temple is one of the 18th-century additions desired by Marcantonio IV to follow the English Romantic fashion of the time (see Giardino del Lago, stop 20). Made of real antique Roman fragments—most of them from the Roman Forum—it was assembled to mimic a ruin. The temple is flanked by two altars with copies of Greek inscriptions.

Taking Via dei Cavalli Marini, you'll reach to your right the:

13. **Casino dell'Orologio.** This lovely, picturesque structure with its soaring tower was the modest dwelling of the villa's gardener. Don't be too jealous, because he was ejected in 1791, when the pavilion was turned into a museum for the sculptures the Borghese family excavated at the ancient Roman site of Gabii, a Roman town about 15 miles east of Rome. The portico and tower with the clock were added then, but the museum had a brief life: In 1807 most of the collection was "requisitioned" by Napoleon and now resides in the Louvre. Currently under restoration, this pavilion will become a museum again, housing 150 original marble statues that have been removed from the park to protect them from weather

The *Ottobrata* in Villa Borghese

It was part of the paternalistic system then ruling the city that the rich and powerful families bestowed their protection and riches on the people on special occasions. Poverty was widespread in the 18th and 19th century, and these occasional gifts were very welcome to Romans.

Grape harvesting in October was one such occasion, when Rome's most powerful families opened their villas to the people. Called the *Ottobrata,* it was a celebration lasting several days. Those organized at Villa Pinciana, as the park was then called, by the Borghese princes were particularly famous. The people could use the gardens and woods, while the jet set of the time was invited to receptions in the luxurious pavilions *(casini).* Shows—including theater and concerts—as well as carousels (real ones, on real horses) were offered to entertain the people, and wine was freely distributed. Evenings ended with the dance of the *sartarello* (a traditional dance) and sometimes fireworks. So popular was the event that the army had to be called in to keep order and help with the huge carriage traffic jams. For the famous *Ottobrata* of 1842, the most grandiose of all, the prince Borghese offered three carousels involving women for the first time (traditionally ladies did not ride except in carriages), and athletic games and grandiose fireworks at the end of each day.

It is this tradition of hospitality that allowed the government to preserve the villa from developers and transform it into a public park for everybody to enjoy.

damage and vandalism. It should also house a permanent exhibit on the history of the villa, with prints, plans, and photographs showing the transformations it underwent since its creation.

Retracing your steps, take Viale Pietro Canonica, where, immediately to your right is the:

14. **Fortezzuola.** The medieval aspect of the building—and its name, which means "little fortress"—was actually an

18th-century addition to the original 17th-century building. Since 1960 it has housed the **Museo Canonica,** dedicated to the modern sculptor Pietro Canonica who had his studio and residence here from 1927 until 1959, the year of his death. Both his apartment—finely furnished and decorated with 19th-century Piemontese paintings and Flemish tapestries—and his studio are open to the public. The museum is open Tuesday through Saturday from 9am to 7pm, Sunday and holidays from 9am to 1:30pm. Admission is charged. The **Monumento all'Alpino** across from the entrance to the museum is a sculpture by Canonica and a monument to Italy's illustrious mountain troops.

Continuing on, after a few steps and on your left is:

15. **Piazza di Siena.** This elegant space—named after the Borghese family's city of origin—was designed in 1792 following ancient Roman models for a stadium. It was used for shows of various sorts, but especially for horse races, as the main square of Siena. Down to this day it hosts various events, including Rome's **Concorso Ippico Internazionale (International Horse Show)** in May, a wonderful competition that attracts some of the best riders and mounts in the world.

Over the bleachers to the south side of the piazza is the:

16. **Casino di Raffaello (Raphael's Pavilion).** The name is thought to be a misnomer, perhaps a confusion with another pavilion located in the Galoppatoio (see below). Raphael's Pavilion was built in the 16th century and transformed in 1791 by the addition of the **Church of the Immacolata** (inside is the tomb of the sculptor Pietro Canonica; see stop 14). The building was used as a private residence until recently and is currently under restoration. The plan is to convert it into a children's museum with playrooms and activities.

Beyond, Viale d. Casina di Raffaello opens onto a space graced to the left by the:

17. **Tempio di Diana (Temple of Diana).** This very elegant domed construction was built in 1789 by Mario Asprucci, following the canons of classical architecture. The original

ancient Roman statue of Diana that decorated the interior and gave its name to the temple was removed.

Outside the temple, farther toward the left, you can see between the trees a statue. It is the one to Umberto I, erected in 1925; semihidden away by vegetation, it stands as a reminder of the failed attempt of the Savoy kings to rename the Villa Borghese.

Retrace your steps to Viale Pietro Canonica, cross it and take Via del Lago. To your right is the:

18. **Fontana dei Mascheroni (Fountain of Masks).** All the elements of this composition—including the Tritons at the corner—were sculpted in the 16th century after a design by Giacomo della Porta for the Fontana del Moro in Piazza Navona (see Walking Tour 2). Removed in 1874 from that fountain, they were later used here, but instead of being all grouped together, the Tritons were located on their own small basin away from the main fountain.

Across Via del Lago to your left is another fountain:

19. **Fonte Gaia,** a unique design with a marble base carved with rabbit heads and decorated with a sculpture by Giovanni Nicolini from 1929, depicting a family of satyrs. It's a celebration of life (if a little weird).

Continuing on Via del Lago you enter the:

20. **Giardino del Lago (Lake Garden).** This garden was created at the end of the 18th century for Marcantonio IV using part of the hunting grounds of the park; he wanted an English-style garden—the height of fashion at the time—and, in accordance with the family tradition, the best and most elegant in Rome. In addition to the architects Antonio and Mario Asprucci and various gardeners, he called in the British painter Jacob Moore and used antique marble and statues from the Borghese family's collection to decorate it. They created a body of water for him—commonly referred to as the *laghetto* (small lake) by locals—immersed in thick vegetation including a great variety of exotic spices, and interspersed with antiquities and fake ruins and temples. Although the lake is really diminutive, you can rent rowboats—an activity very popular with locals and children of all ages—to see the decor up close and meet the ducks and swans.

Take a Break   Before you get to the lake, you'll find the cafe and snack bar of the Giardino del Lago, housed in an octagonal small building. You can have a welcome refreshment here, but don't expect it to be cheap.

Overlooking the lake in perfect Romantic style is the:

21. **Temple of Aesculapius,** built on a little island. Inside is a statue of Aesculapius, god of medicine, while the upper level is decorated with other antique statues and carvings depicting related figures.

    Continuing on past the lake is the:

22. **Arco di Settimio Severo (Arch of Septimius Severus).** This fake Roman arch was added in the 19th century to mark the entrance to the Giardino del Lago. It is decorated on top with an antique statue of the emperor Septimius Severus (now a copy), flanked by two prisoners.

    Pass under the arch and continue on to your right to the majestic staircase opening to your right that is decorated with fountains. Down the stairs and across Viale delle Belle Arti is the:

23. **Palazzo delle Belle Arti,** built between 1908 and 1911 for the International Expo. Since 1915 this beautiful building has housed the **Galleria Nazionale d'Arte Moderna e Contemporanea,** with a broad collection focusing mainly (but not solely) on Italian artists from the 19th and the 20th centuries. It is open Tuesday through Sunday from 8:30am to 7:30pm. Admission is charged.

    Take a Break   Il **Caffè delle Arti,** opening on Via Gramsci, is the elegant cafe and snack bar of GNAM (Gallery of Modern Art), where you can have coffee, tea, or a light meal and, if you are lucky, listen to some live jazz or classical music.

Walk along Via Bernadotte, lined with statues of famous poets and writers from around the world, donated by their various governments. Once in Piazzale del Fiocco, note the 19th-century fountain dedicated to Aesculapius. Turn left onto Viale Fiorello La Guardia, named for New York City's most famous mayor. Passing the **Propilei Egizi**—a monumental 19th-century work in Egyptian style—you will find to your left the:

24. **Aranciera (Orangery).** This building was once the Casino dei Giuochi d'Acqua, the most elegant in the villa and a favorite location for parties and balls. In 1849 the building was devastated by battles during the Republican upheaval, and what you see today is how it was reconstructed. It owes its name to the citrus fruit that used to be stored in part of the building after the fruit harvest in the park's gardens.

Continuing on and again to your left is the:

25. **Portico dei Leoni.** Created by Antonio Asprucci in the 18th century as a part of the Romantic English garden, it was completed in the 19th century by Luigi Canina. A sort of grotto faced by a fountain, it houses fragments of ancient Roman inscriptions and carvings. The gates are a recent addition made in an attempt to protect the contents from theft and vandalism, since some of the carvings had been stolen and the walls defaced with graffiti (now restored).

You will find yourself now in Piazzale delle Canestre; to your left is the:

26. **Mostra dell'Acqua Felice,** the monumental fountain marking the arrival of the aqueduct built by Giovanni Fontana in 1610 to bring water to the villa. This is the only surviving section of that aqueduct, which was destroyed by the bombardments of 1849; some of the decorations were added in the 18th century.

Also to your left is the:

27. **Globe Theatre.** This is a faithful replica of Shakespeare's Globe Theatre. The original was built in 1599 by Richard and Cuthbert Burbage on the south side of the Thames, and became the permanent home of Shakespeare's company (the Chamberlain's, and later King's Men) where he first presented all his greatest plays. The most popular theatre in London, its design became a model for later theaters throughout the 17th century. It burned in 1613 and was rebuilt in 1614, but it was pulled down in 1644 for the residential development of the area. What is it doing in Rome, you ask? Romans have always been glad to borrow the best of other cultures. The Toti Globe Theatre in Villa Borghese performs not only Shakespeare, but many

other playwrights' works as well (Largo Aqua Felix, entrance at Piazzale delle Ginestre).

To your right is Viale delle Magnolie, where Romans of all ages learn to skate. Its name comes from the magnolia trees that lined this long alley that runs through the 1908 viaduct and connects Villa Borghese with the Gardens of the Pincio. The busts along the alley also date from that time; they were commissioned and placed to smooth the transition between the two gardens, since the alleys of the Pincio (see Walking Tour 4) were lined with busts of famous Italians. Next to Viale delle Magnolie is the alley leading to the:

28. **Galoppatoio.** What is now a horse-training ring was once the Villetta Doria, an elegant building decorated by Raphael and surrounded by a perfect English garden. The Borghese acquired it in 1831 when it was already in quite bad shape; in 1849 it was completely destroyed by the French bombardments. Luckily, Raphael's frescoes had already been detached and removed in 1836. The building had already turned into a horse stable and ring by the end of the 19th century.

There you'll also see another surprising sight, a huge:

29. **Anchored hot-air balloon.** This is a very recent addition to the facilities of the villa. Established as a temporary installation for the celebrations of the new millennium, it seems to have become a permanent feature. The balloon is decorated with an exact replica of the drawings of the first balloon used by the Montgolfier brothers in 1783. Although it is firmly attached with a safety cable to the ground, soaring into the air is an exhilarating experience that offers excellent views of the ground. From these heights you can discover all kind of things that are usually hidden by high walls, such as the gardens of Palazzo del Quirinale. The balloon operates daily from 9:30am to sunset (flights are suspended in bad weather). Admission is charged.

Also starting from Piazzale delle Canestre, Viale Goethe branches off to the right into Viale San Paolo del Brasile—the monument to Wolfgang Goethe is to your left. Continuing on Viale San Paolo del Brasile you will reach, to your left, the:

30. **Casina delle Rose,** one of the most famous in the park. This 18th-century building was purchased by the Borghese in 1833; they had it restored by Luigi Canina and integrated into the villa. In later years, it was turned into a trattoria; the cuisine there was so good that Gioacchino Belli—a famous Roman poet—celebrated it in his writings. Not all good things last forever, and after the trattoria closed down, the building was turned into stables where cows were kept. This inglorious role was only a brief parenthesis, though. After the Second World War, the Casina found its way back to celebrity when it was turned into a dance hall that became a hip spot of the Roman *dolce vita*. Completely abandoned in the 1970s, it was in ruins when restorations began (again) in 2002. At this writing, works have been mostly completed and the building should soon contain exhibits and shows dedicated to the movie world.

Exit the villa by Viale San Paolo del Brasile; you'll find yourself at **Porta Pinciana,** one of the original Roman city gates in the walls built by emperor Aurelius in the 3rd century A.D. Make sure you pay attention crossing the street here; traffic is fast along the thoroughfare that descends to Piazzale Flaminio below. One of the subway entrances to the Metro station Piazza di Spagna is there, too.

Monti

Start: Metro stop Repubblica.

Finish: Metro stop Colosseo.

Time: 2 hours excluding museum visits and other activities.

Best Time: Daytime Tuesday through Sunday when the museums and churches are open.

Worst Time: Nighttime and Monday when the museums are closed; midday during the week, when churches are closed.

The "high country" of Rome is the Monti district, which encompasses several of the city's famous seven hills and the saddle of land between them. If you had a relief map of the area, you would see the "mounts" of Monti: the Viminale, part of the Esquilino, and part of the Quirinale hills. Monti encompasses a large section of what was Republican Rome (the 5th c. B.C. onward), when the patrician families built their homes atop these hills. To the southwest, the hills slope down to a valley that was known in ancient times as the *Subura,* which meant "area beneath the city." This was a zone of more humble dwellings for the lower classes that lay between the hills and the great public buildings of the Forum (see Walking Tour 1).

Beginning at the time of Constantine, several basilicas were built in Monti (the queen of them all is Santa Maria Maggiore; see stop 7). At the time of the barbarian invasions, Rome's aqueducts were cut and Monti was deprived of water. Hence after the fall of the Roman Empire, Monti was one of the areas of the city that became depopulated and was largely reclaimed by nature. There was a resurgence in the medieval period, however, when Monti was fortified and protective towers were erected to guard the access roads to Rome and also the Subura, where the population had congregated. In fact, most of Rome's still extant medieval towers are in Monti. Pope Sixtus V later built a new aqueduct to bring water to the area, which enabled the repopulation of the higher elevations of Monti.

With the rise of the papal state, the great papal palace on the nearby Quirinal Hill was built as a holiday residence for the pontiff. Construction began in 1573 under Pope Gregory XIII and continued for decades. (The magnificent Quirinal palace passed to the royal family after the unification of Italy in 1870 under the house of Savoy; today it is the home of the president of the Italian republic.) A few grand residences were erected by Rome's nobility starting in the 16th century in neighboring Monti, but in general, this part of Rome remained somewhat aloof or apart from the bustling heart of Renaissance Rome. It was a comparatively quiet area of monasteries, churches, and cloisters.

After unification, Monti saw great changes, as Via Nazionale was cut through the old neighborhood and the Esquiline Hill was developed as an area of apartment buildings. Via Cavour was also created and lined with 19th-century *palazzi,* but in the streets behind these modern avenues the older dwellings and little alleys remain.

This itinerary begins in what is not strictly speaking the *rione* (officially designated neighborhood or borough) of Monti, but takes advantage of the nearby subway stops to provide a glimpse of a few other treasures of Rome and indeed, some of its most recognizable buildings. Also, although Monti is a hilly area, most of the time on this itinerary you will find yourself descending.

• • • • • • • • • • • • • • • •

Monti

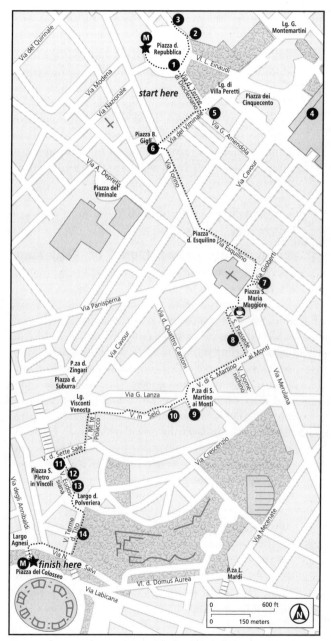

Leave the subway at the Repubblica Metro station, and exit into:

1. **Piazza della Repubblica.** You will notice on the south side of this semicircular piazza two large complexes of buildings with curved facades that mimic the shape of the piazza. These neoclassical buildings went up in 1887–98. Standing with your back to these buildings, you can appreciate the beautiful fountain with bronze nymphs riding sea monsters (1888) in the center of the piazza—though between you and it will be, unfortunately, dozens of buzzing buses, cars, and motorbikes, as this is a very busy intersection.

   Across the piazza loom some large, brick, antique-looking structures. These are in fact the remains of the:

2. **Terme di Diocleziano (Baths of Diocletian).** Diocletian is an interesting emperor for several reasons. His reign was long (A.D. 284–305), after which he abdicated and lived for years in retirement (instead of being murdered, as was the fate of many an emperor). Strangest of all, this Roman emperor probably only visited Rome once, preferring instead to leave the western half of the empire in the hands of Maximianus, the notoriously brutal general he made his coemperor (and whose career met a far more violent end than Diocletian's). Diocletian governed the eastern provinces of the empire from his magnificent palace in Dalmatia (in today's Croatia). However, Diocletian did give the Romans this once-awesome and now-ruined structure. To get an idea of how enormous these baths were, you have to imagine that the entire western half of Piazza della Repubblica was once the *esedra*—the exercise hemicycle—of the complex, which extended all the way to Via del Viminale to the south and Piazza San Bernardo to the north. Actually, the church of San Bernardo alle Terme in Piazza San Bernardo was built using the round structure marking the outer corner of the baths. The *calidarium* or hot room of the baths started just east of the fountain on Piazza della Repubblica. The baths could accommodate 3,000 people.

   The part of the baths directly across the piazza was transformed into the church of:

3. **Santa Maria degli Angeli.** This church occupies what were the bath's central and most imposing halls, as well as what was the *tepidarium* (warm area), the room placed between the *frigidarium* (cool area) and *calidarium* (sauna). The original Renaissance plan included a church and an attached monastery with two cloisters, and was designed by Michelangelo, who sensitively tried to preserve as much of the original structures as possible. In the 18th century, the church was enlarged and redecorated by Luigi Vanvitelli. Part of a former monastery attached to the church has been converted into a museum that contains a famous epigraphy collection: It gathers together various inscriptions that have been found in archaeological sites all over Rome, mostly carved in stone. Admission is charged.

Cross the piazza if you wish to visit either of these sights. Otherwise, turn to your right and walk along Via delle Terme di Diocleziano. In the distance, you will see a huge modern-looking building; you may have visited it already, for this is the:

4. **Stazione Termini,** the main train station of Rome. Recently the subject of a multiyear renovation, it contains not only the train station but also a bookstore, supermarket, restaurants, and shops. Most people (and some guidebooks) consider it an example of Fascist architecture, but that isn't strictly correct. Although the original plan was drawn up in 1938, it was never completed. After World War II another design competition was held, and the station finally opened in the Jubilee year 1950.

At the corner of Via delle Terme di Diocleziano and Via Viminale is the:

5. **Palazzo Massimo alle Terme,** a museum that was founded in 1889 but has been completely restored and reorganized. Its stunning collection of ancient Roman art includes a famous **satyr pouring wine,** a Roman copy of an original by Greek sculptor Praxiteles; the ***Daughter of Niobe*** from the Gardens of Sallust; and an ***Apollo*** copied from an original by another Greek sculptor, Phidias. The collection includes literally hundreds of works, including an interesting series showing how the style of representation changed under various emperors. The upper level

holds a magnificent collection of **floor mosaics,** including many large ones, that once graced some of the most elegant villas in ancient Rome. Here you'll also find a Roman **fresco collection,** including those from the **Villa of Livia** on the Palatine Hill. Admission is charged.

Turn right on Via Viminale and head downhill. In a few blocks, at the corner of Via Torino on the right is the:

6. **Teatro dell' Opera,** Rome's opera house. It was built in 1878–80 and restored and redesigned in 1926–28 and again in 1958. The result is a rather drab, modern exterior (the entrance was moved around to the side of the building). The theater was originally known as the Teatro Costanzi, after the builder, Domenico Costanzi, who built it with his own money. When the city of Rome failed to pay him for the work, he began operating the theater himself, and with some success. Puccini's *Tosca* premiered here in January 1900, and it hosted other important first nights as well.

   Turn left on Via Torino. A short walk will bring you to **Piazza dell' Esquilino,** which feels more like a big intersection than a public square. It is dominated on the left by the back of the Basilica of Santa Maria Maggiore. Bear left along the north side of the church, which will bring you to:

7. **Piazza Santa Maria Maggiore,** on the west side of which is this grand and storied basilica. It has undergone many changes over the centuries, but Santa Maria Maggiore remains one of Rome's four great basilicas. It was built as a sanctuary for Mary (mother of Jesus) and was originally referred to as Santa Maria della Neve (St. Mary of the Snow) because, the legend goes, its outline was drawn in the snow that had miraculously fallen in the summer of A.D. 352. The current baroque facade dates from more than 1,000 years after that, however; it was designed by Ferdinando Fuga, who sandwiched it between two palaces that were built around the church in the 17th and 18th centuries. But behind the facade, much older sections of the church remain. The walls are original, as are the mosaics of the apse and side walls. Although restored, the floors are the original 12th-century cosmatesque style (a mosaic of marble and colored stones).

The 15th-century coffered wooden ceiling is covered in gold—said to be the first gold brought back from the Americas and donated by the Spanish queen. In the loggia, the **13th-century mosaics** of the old facade are preserved. Santa Maria Maggiore is also the last resting place of the great **Giovanni Lorenzo Bernini** (his tomb is to the right side of the altar). The basilica also contains a little-known work of Michelangelo, the **Cappella Sforza,** which he designed but did not complete.

Now might be a good time to:

☕ Take a Break On the southeast side of Piazza Santa Maria Maggiore sits the cafe **Bar Gelateria Molinaro** (Piazza Santa Maria Maggiore 12A; ✆ **06/ 4746612**). They make a particularly good cup of espresso—and the gelato is good, too.

Now with your back to the basilica's facade, cross the square and take the small street to the right of the large Via Merulana. This little street (Via S. Prassede) leads to:

8. **Basilica di Santa Prassede.** It seems odd to call a church that has existed on this site for over 1,200 years one of Rome's best-kept secrets, but there it is: There has been a place of worship on this spot since at least A.D. 489. Santa Prassede also contains the most outstanding remaining work of Byzantine art in all of Rome—the chapel of San Zenone, which was created by Pope Pasquale I (817–24) as a mausoleum for his mother. The floor is made from polychrome marble; the mosaics in the walls and ceiling represent Christ surrounded by angels, as well as various saints. In the main nave, the arch over the altar and the apse are decorated with glittering mosaics of variegated color and gold, dating from the 9th century. In the center is Christ, and to the left Saint Paul and Santa Prassede, as well as Pasquale I, who offers the gift of the church. Although an amazing amount of artwork from the first millennium is still intact here, other parts of Santa Prassede were redone in later centuries. The ever-present Giovanni Lorenzo Bernini left his mark here as well: Look for his early bust of Bishop G. B. Santoni (1614) by the third column to the right in the main nave.

Exiting Santa Prassede, turn right and continue down Via Santa Prassede to Via S. Martino ai Monti. Turn right on Via S. Martino ai Monti, which is actually the ancient "clivus Suburanus," the road that led down into the Subura. At number 20A, a plaque commemorates the fact that the Bolognese painter Domenichino (1581–1641) once lived here. Continuing on, the street opens into the:

9. **Piazza di San Martino ai Monti,** named for the church that you will see to your left. This is another of the ancient basilicas of Monti. This site dates from the late 5th century; however, unlike Santa Prassede, most traces of the early church have been erased. The door that you see facing the piazza dates from 16th century; the entrance was later reoriented, and is around the block on Viale del Monte Oppio. Although the current form and decoration of the church date from the reconstruction of 1636, through the crypt you can gain access to **the aula,** a paleo-Christian place of worship that dates from the 3rd century. Some pieces of Roman and medieval stonework remain, as well as remnants of 9th-century frescoes and a 6th-century mosaic.

On the south side of the Piazza di San Martino ai Monti is the imposing **Torre dei Capocci,** one of the medieval towers of the Monti neighborhood. It is 36m (118 ft.) high (you can't visit the inside, however). The second, shorter tower is known as the Torre dei Graziani.

Two streets exit the piazza to the south; take the smaller one to the left, the Via in Selci. This is the continuation of the ancient "clivus Suburanus," descending into the Subura. Number 82 Via in Selci is an Augustinian monastery. Inside the entrance is an atrium, at the back of which and on the left-hand side is the church of:

10. **Santa Lucia in Selci,** whose current facade was designed by Carlo Maderno and dates from 1604. It is decorated inside with paintings by Cavalier d'Arpino (*God the Father* and Saints Augustine and Monica), as well as works by Borromini. Maderno himself designed the ciborium, which is decorated with polychrome marble and statues in alabaster and gold.

Continue on Via in Selci until you reach the 18th-century church of **Saints Gioacchino e Anna ai Monti.**

Turn left just after the church and walk along its side until you come to a flight of steps. These lead up to Via delle Sette Sale. Turn right, and a short walk will bring you to:

11. **Piazza San Pietro in Vincoli.** As you enter the piazza, you will see to your right the **Torre dei Margani,** which dates from the 12th century and was traditionally (but incorrectly) said to have belonged to Rome's notorious Borgia family. It was later turned into a bell tower for the church of **San Francesco di Paola,** which is the Calabrese church in Rome, built in the 17th century (it is reached by a flight of steps going down from the piazza to the right).

To your left is the church for which the piazza is named:

12. **Basilica di San Pietro in Vincoli (Saint Peter in Chains).** The church is sometimes called Saint Peter Eudossiana, after Eudossia, the wife of the emperor Valetinian III. The legend is that Eudossia received from her mother the chains that had held Saint Peter during his imprisonment in Jerusalem. When Pope Leo the Great (440–61) brought this chain together with the chains that held Peter in Rome, the two miraculously fused. This church was built to hold the relic. Beneath the church, archaeological explorations have found remains of a 3rd-century house with an *aula* (before the conversion of Constantine, Christians met in secret in private houses). Like most churches in Rome, San Pietro in Vincoli has been altered and reconstructed many times. The portico is from the 15th century. Inside, 20 ancient marble columns line the main nave; the coffered ceiling is from the 18th century.

The artist most associated with the church is Michelangelo. In the right transept is his elaborate mausoleum for **Pope Julius II,** which he was unable to finish because the succeeding pope (Leo X) transferred him to other projects. The mausoleum's masterpiece is Michelangelo's great sculpture of **Moses,** which he began in 1514. The seated Moses is depicted in the moment when he returns from Mount Sinai and finds, to his disgust, that his people have returned to idolatry in his absence. If you think it looks like Moses is sporting horns, you're right. This oddity is thought to be the result of an incorrect translation found in the Latin (Vulgate) Bible used in Michelangelo's time. St. Jerome, who produced the Vulgate, misinterpreted the Hebrew word for "light," thus robbing Moses of his halo and giving him a set of horns. There are other treasures in the church as well, including a Byzantine mosaic (circa A.D. 600) of a bearded St. Sebastian, and paintings by Domenichino and Guercino.

If you exit the church and turn to your left on Via Eudossiana, you come immediately to the:

13. **Engineering School** of the University of Rome, which is interesting to nonengineers because it is actually housed in the former convent of the basilica. If you enter, in front of you and to the left is the charming **cloister,** built in the beginning of the 16th century. The convent's original well is at the center.

Continue to the end of Via Eudossiana into Largo della Polveriera. Bear left, and then turn right on Via Terme di Tito. Along this street to your left are the few remains of the:

14. **Terme di Tito,** the thermal baths built by the emperor Tito over Nero's Domus Aurea (see Walking Tour 1) and opened in A.D. 80.

Via Terme di Tito dead-ends into Via Nicola Salvi. Turn right, and walk along Via Nicola Salvi to Largo Agnesi, which affords a great view of the **Colosseum,** the **Arch of Constantine,** and other Roman ruins (see Walking Tour 1). From the bottom end of Largo Agnesi, you can take a flight of steps down to the Piazza del Colosseo. You will find yourself right in front of the Colosseo Metro stop.

Essentials & Recommended Reading

Rome can be quite overwhelming at first sight, with the noise and the confusion that seems to reign almost everywhere, but in reality it is a surprisingly easy city to get around once you have figured out the public transportation. Also, Romans are very welcoming to visitors and will go out of their way to help a foreigner in difficulty; you don't even need to ask. Usually if they see you poring over a map, someone will certainly come and ask you if you need assistance.

TOURIST INFORMATION

You'll find Rome's central tourist office in Via Parigi 5 (© 06/488991; www.romaturismo.it; Mon–Sat 9am–7pm); they also maintain a desk at the international arrivals in the Terminal B of Fiumicino Airport (daily 8am–7pm).

The most convenient, though, are the tourist information kiosks scattered around the center of the city (all of them are open daily 9am–6pm). You'll find them at:

- **Castel Sant'Angelo** (Piazza Pia; ✆ **06/68809707**)
- **Largo Goldoni** (Via del Corso at Via Condotti; ✆ **06/68136061**)
- **Piazza delle Cinque Lune** (off Piazza Navona; ✆ **06/68809240**)
- **Fori Imperiali** (Piazza Tempio della Pace; ✆ **06/69924307**)
- **Santa Maria Maggiore** (Via dell'Olmata; ✆ **06/4740955**)
- **Stazione Termini** (in front of the railroad station, ✆ **06/47825194;** inside the gallery, ✆ **06/48906300**)
- **Trastevere** (Piazza Sonnino; ✆ **06/58333457**)
- **San Giovanni** (Piazza San Giovanni in Laterano; ✆ **06/77203535**)
- **Fontana di Trevi** (Via Minghetti; ✆ **06/6782988**)
- **Palazzo delle Esposizioni** (Via Nazionale; ✆ **06/47824525**)

The tourist office of the **Vatican** is in Piazza San Pietro (✆ **06/69884466;** open Mon–Sat 8:30am–6pm).

CITY LAYOUT

Most of Rome's historical center lies on the left bank of the River Tevere (Tiber), which meanders in a general north-to-south direction. On the right bank are the Vatican and Trastevere. The major transportation hub is **Stazione Termini,** Rome's main train station, to the east of the city center. From there, **Via Barberini** heads west into **Via Veneto** and **Via del Tritone; Via Nazionale** heads southwest to **Piazza Venezia,** part of the thoroughfare that, through **Via del Plebiscito** and **Corso Vittorio Emanuele II,** reaches **St. Peter's Basilica;** and **Via Cavour** heads south to the **Colosseum** and joins **Via dei Fori Imperiali** and Via Labicana toward **San Giovanni in Laterano.**

MAPS

You'll do well with the free tourist-office map, but even better with a complete map with *stradario* (street directory), which is essential for locating addresses; you can purchase one of these at any newsstand and many bookstores.

GETTING AROUND

Subway

The **subway** (*Metropolitana* or just *Metro*) in Rome is rather limited—only two lines (Linea A and Linea B)—but it is easy to use and the only way to avoid the traffic jams which have been characteristic of the city since ancient Roman times. It runs Sunday through Friday from 5:30am to 11:30pm and Saturday from 5:30am to 12:30am. Stops are equipped with elevators for disabled access except the stations of Colosseo, Circo Massimo, and Cavour on line B.

Motor Scooter

The most common way to get around is by bus *(autobus)*—unless you are daring enough to try a **motor scooter** *(motorino)*, which you can rent at several places in town including **Treno e Scooter** (**TeS;** Via Marsala, outside Stazione Termini, by the taxi stand and subway entrance; ✆ **06/48905823**), and **New Scooter** (Via Quattro Novembre 96, off Piazza Venezia; ✆ **06/6790300**).

Bus

Buses go virtually everywhere and the only thing required is to know which line you need and to have faith that your bus will eventually come. Although hotel personnel, bus drivers, and the local passersby will be happy to volunteer information—sometimes engaging in lively discussions among themselves on which line would be best for you—the huge bus system is rather daunting for a newcomer. You will soon learn, though, the few specific lines of interest to tourists: **23** (from Piazza Risorgimento to Porta Portese and returning along the Lungotevere on the opposite bank of the river); **62** (from Borgo Sant'Angelo near the Vatican to Via Nomentana); **64** (from Termini to St. Peter's station); **87** (from Piazza Cavour by Castel Sant'Angelo to San Giovanni in Laterano); **492** (from Porta Pia to Piazza Risorgimento); **910** (from Termini Station to Via Pinciana by Villa Borghese); and the diminutive electric buses **116** (from Gianicolo to Villa Borghese), **116T** (from Gianicolo to Piazza della Repubblica), **117** (from Piazza del Popolo to San Giovanni in Laterano), and **119** (from Piazza del Popolo to Largo Argentina). To these you can add the entertaining but circuitous **tram** lines **3** (from Villa Giulia to Trastevere station, passing by San Giovanni in Laterano, Circus Maximus, and Colosseum); **8** (from Largo Argentina to Trastevere station); and **19** (from Piazza Risorgimento to Porta Maggiore). Check when you get there, though, because some of the lines may have changed or new ones may have been added. All buses run daily from 5:30am to 12:30am—with varying frequency, more often at rush hours on business days and rarely on Sundays. Some lines stop at 8:30pm and others don't run on Sundays; the few night lines are marked N for *notturno* (night) and run hourly from midnight to 5am.

You'll need to buy tickets in advance (valid on all public transportation)—from vending machines at some bus stops, ticket booths in a Metro station, most bars and tobacconist shops, and newsstands—and **stamp** them upon boarding. Regular tickets are valid for 75 minutes on multiple rides (only one subway ride, though), but you can also get daily, 3-day, and weekly passes if you are planning to use a lot of public transportation.

Taxis

Otherwise, **taxis** are an excellent way to avoid headaches and travel in comfort. Rates are reasonable enough to make it worth it. The only catch—yes there is one here too—is that they don't cruise the streets as in most U.S. cities, but wait at taxi stands. To get a taxi you need to summon one by telephone or walk to one of the many stands scattered in Rome. Here are the most important: **Piazza Barberini, Piazza della Cancelleria, Vicolo del Gallinaccio, Piazza San Silvestro, Piazza Santi Apostoli,** and **Via G. Zanardelli** in the Centro; **Piazza del Risorgimento** near St. Peter's Basilica; **Piazza G. G. Belli** and **Piazza Mastai** in Trastevere. If there isn't a car when you arrive, just wait by the pole marked TAXI, or call the 24-hour radio taxi service at ☎ **06/88177,** 06/6645, or 06/4994.

FAST FACTS   Rome

American Express   You'll find them at Piazza di Spagna 38 (☎ **06/67641;** Mon–Fri 9am–5:30pm, Sat 9am–12:30pm, closed major local holy days).

Area Codes   The area code for Rome and surroundings is 06 (you need to dial this area code even for local calls from within

Rome). From the U.S. dial 011; then the country code for Italy, 39; then the area code 06 (keep the zero); followed by the local number. Note that phone numbers can have almost any number of digits, from five up to eight. Cellular phones have the area code of the company that provides the service (these are three-digit numbers, such as 337). Toll-free numbers usually have the 800 area code, and paying services often have 900.

ATMs   You'll find ATMs everywhere in town. The only hitch is that most are linked to the Cirrus network (the least common in the U.S.) and few to the Plus network (the most common in the U.S.); among those linked to PLUS is **BNL (Banca Nazionale del Lavoro),** but ask your bank for a list of locations before leaving on your trip.

Automobile Club   **Automobile Club d'Italia (ACI)** assists motorists in Italy. Dial ⓒ **06/4477** for 24-hour information and ⓒ **116** for **road emergencies.**

Babysitters   Few hotels in Rome offer structured activities for children, but most have agreements with professional babysitting agencies such as **Giorgi Tiziana** (Via Cavour 295; ⓒ **06/ 4742564**), and **GED** (Via Sicilia 166/b; ⓒ **06/42012495;** www.gedonline.it).

Business Hours   Shops are open Monday through Saturday from 8:30am to 1pm and 4 to 7:30pm. Groceries and other food shops are closed Thursday afternoons and clothing and shoe shops on Monday mornings. Offices open Monday through Friday 8:30am to 1pm and 2:30 to 5:30pm, while most banks are open Monday through Friday 8:30am to 1:30pm and 2:30 to 4pm (some banks 3–4:30pm).

Credit Cards   For lost or stolen cards contact: American Express (ⓒ **06/7220348,** 06/72282, or 06/72461; www. americanexpress.it); Diners Club (ⓒ **800/864064866** toll-free within Italy; www.dinersclub.com); MasterCard (ⓒ **800/ 870866** toll-free within Italy; www.mastercard.com); or Visa (ⓒ **800/819014** toll-free within Italy; www.visaeu.com).

Currency Exchange   Exchange bureaus (marked *cambio/change/ wechsel*) are scattered in the center of Rome; usually you'll get the best rates at points of entry such as Termini train stations and Fiumicino airport.

Doctors Embassies and consulates keep a list of English-speaking doctors and dentists; the concierge at your hotel can also recommend a doctor.

Electricity Electricity in Rome is 220 volts and plugs have round prongs. You can buy an adapter kit in many electronics stores before you leave or at any *ferramenta* (hardware store) after you arrive.

Embassies & Consulates The United States (℃ 06/46741), Canada (℃ 06/445981), Australia (℃ 06/852721), New Zealand (℃ 06/4402928), United Kingdom (℃ 06/74825441), and Ireland (℃ 06/6979121) all maintain a 24-hour assistance service.

Emergencies Call ℃ **118** for an **ambulance,** ℃ **115** for the **fire department,** ℃ **113** or 112 for the **police,** and ℃ **116** for **road emergencies.**

Hospitals **Santo Spirito** (Lungotevere in Sassia 1; ℃ **06/68351,** or 06/68352241 for first aid); and **Fatebenefratelli** (Piazza Fatebenefratelli 2 on the Isola Tiberina; ℃ **06/68371,** or 06/6837299 for first aid) are the most central.

Hot Lines Call ℃ **06/3054343** or 06/490663 for drug abuse. Call ℃ **1 9696** toll free for the Children's Hot Line (Telefono Azzurro); adolescents and adults can call ℃ 199151515. You can get information 24/7 on nearly anything in four languages including English at the tourist information hot line at ℃ **06/36004399.**

Internet Access & Cybercafes **Easy Everything** (Piazza Barberini 2) is open 24 hours a day 7 days a week and has 350 computers. **Internet Train** (Via Pastini 125, near the Pantheon; Via delle Fornaci 3, near San Pietro; Via Merry del Val 20 [friendly English- and Spanish-speaking staff], in Trastevere; and Via in Arcione 103, by Fontana di Trevi).

Liquor Laws It is forbidden to disturb the *quiete pubblica* (public quiet) and litter, including getting drunk and loud. It's also illegal to drink a can of beer while sitting on a ruin or a fountain wall.

Mail The notoriously unreliable Italian mail of the old days seems to have become something of the past, and *Posta Prioritaria* (express/priority) will get a letter to the U.S. in 4 to 5 days for .80€ ($1). Postcards without envelopes and all mail put in the wrong mailbox (the red one for local mail instead of the blue ones for international mail) will still take forever.

Lots of tourists like using the Vatican post office by St. Peter's Basilica in Rome; same price, maybe a bit faster, and with unique Holy See stamps (which work only from the blue mailboxes by the Vatican post office).

Pharmacies Regular opening hours are Monday through Saturday 8:30am to 1pm and 4 to 7:30pm, but on rotation, one will be open after hours in each neighborhood (the name of the open ones is posted on the door of the closed ones). Usually open at nights are Piazza dei Cinquecento 49, at Termini Station (© **06/4880019**); Via Cola di Rienzo 213 (© **06/3244476**); Piazza Risorgimento 44 (© **06/39738166**); Via Arenula 73 (© **06/68803278**); Corso Rinascimento 50 (© **06/68803985**); Piazza Barberini 49 (© **06/4871195**); or Viale Trastevere 229 (© **06/5882273**).

Police You can reach the police by dialing © **113** or 112.

Post Office You'll find the main post office in Piazza San Silvestro 19 (© **800/160000** toll free within Italy); it is open Monday through Friday 8:30am to 6:30pm and Saturday 8:30am to 1pm.

Restrooms There are a few public toilets (outside the Colosseum; halfway up the steps from Piazza del Popolo to the Pincio; under St. Peter Basilica's colonnade), where the attendant will expect a tip. Bars and cafes have bathrooms only for their customers: Buy a cup of coffee or a glass of mineral water.

Safety The one big danger in Rome is pickpockets, which are particularly active on public transportation and wherever there are crowds. Another danger is getting run over by a moped or a car: Be extremely careful crossing the street, even on clearly marked crosswalks.

Pretty young women traveling alone will attract men's attention and while this is not dangerous, their reactions might be unpleasant. Ignore them as long as it is feasible and otherwise ask any man or woman older than yourself for help. If you dress very differently from the locals, change into more appropriate clothing.

Smoking Smoking is forbidden in all public places except those that can provide a separate area for smokers, such as larger restaurants, clubs, and cafes. Keep it in mind if smoking is important to you.

Street Crossing   Traffic rules are different in Italy than in the U.S. and the U.K. While pedestrians have the right of way when crossing on a crosswalk, they should cause a minimum traffic interruption; wait for a lull. Cars will often barely slow down and instead, just aim a bit away from you. At traffic lights, turning cars and *motorini* (scooters) should give the right of way to the crossing pedestrians that have a green light, but they rarely do. The traffic situation is getting out of hand in Rome and crossing busy streets has become extremely dangerous (accidents are unfortunately frequent). We have only two words for you: Be careful.

Taxes   VAT (value-added tax) is already added in whatever you buy; as a tourist, you can get a refund at the airport for large purchases over 300€; ask the shop attendant for a VAT refund form.

Taxis   You can reach radio taxi by calling © 06/88177, 06/6645, 06/4994, 06/5551, or 06/6545. You can also walk to a taxi station: **Piazza Barberini, Piazza della Cancelleria, Vicolo del Gallinaccio, Piazza San Silvestro, Piazza Santi Apostoli,** and **Via G. Zanardelli** in the Centro; **Piazza del Risorgimento** near St. Peter's Basilica; **Piazza G. G. Belli** and **Piazza Mastai** in Trastevere.

Telephone   To place a call from a public pay phone you'll need to buy a *carta telefonica* (telephone card) from any *tabacchi* (tobacconist), most bars, and newsstands for a preset value (2.60€–7.75€/$3.35–$10). Remember to tear off the perforated corner before inserting your card in the slot, and to dial the area code (see area code in this section). Local calls cost .10€ (15¢).

The international access code from Rome is **00**. To call abroad dial 00, then the country code of the country that you're calling (1 for the United States and Canada, 44 for the United Kingdom, 353 for Ireland, 61 for Australia, 64 for New Zealand) and then the phone number. A cheaper option for calling your home might be using your own calling card, if you have one; check with your calling card provider before leaving on your trip. You can also make collect calls: Dial © 800/1724444 for AT&T; © 800/905825 for MCI; and

☏ 800/172405 or 800/172406 for Sprint; or, to make a collect call to a country other than the United States, dial ☏ 170. Dial ☏ 12 for free directory assistance within Italy, and ☏ 176 for international directory assistance (toll call).

Time Zone   Italy is 1 hour past Greenwich Mean Time and 6 hours ahead of Eastern Standard Time in the United States. Daylight saving starts on the last Sunday in March and ends on the last Sunday in October.

Tipping   Your restaurant bill usually includes 10% to 15% service charge (check the menu, if it is not included you'll have to add it to your bill), but it is customary to leave an additional 5% to 10% if you appreciated the meal. Bars expect a 5% tip at the counter and a 10% to 15% tip at a table. Bellhops will expect about 1€ ($1.30) per bag; you should leave a small tip for the maid in your hotel; taxis expect 10% to 15% of the fare.

Transit Info   **ATAC** (☏ **800/431784** or 06/46952027; www. atac.roma.it), Rome's public transportation authority, is responsible for all bus, tram, and subway service. For railroad information call **Trenitalia** (☏ **06/892021;** www.trenitalia.it).

RECOMMENDED READING

No matter what kind of book you favor, you are likely to find one on Rome—if not as the subject, at least as the background. There are even comic books with Rome as a subject. Nonfiction offerings are abundant, from **Polybius,** the Greek historian who was a hostage in Rome for 16 years during the 2nd century B.C. (*Histories,* reprint Regnery/Gateway 1987 as *Polybius on Roman Imperialism* and Penguin 1980 as *The Rise of the Roman Empire*), to the Roman historian **Tacitus** (*Annals,* Penguin classics series 1956 as *The Annals of Imperial Rome*), to Edward Gibbon's *History of the Decline and Fall of the Roman Empire* (reprint Penguin, abridged version [1983] in paperback)—among the forbidden books of the Catholic church until recent years.

Lighter and often amusing are the reports of travelers from past centuries, such as **Johann Wolfgang von Goethe**'s *Italian Journey* (1816; reprinted by Penguin Books, 1992), and **Stendhal**'s *Three Italian Chronicles* (1826–29; reprint New Directions Publishing, 1991), both containing a large section on Rome. Often hilarious, **Tobias Smollett**'s *Travels through*

France and Italy (Oxford, 1999), first published in 1766, deals in part with the Eternal City. Smollett is so cranky and bad-tempered that it led **Laurence Sterne** to satirize him as the Learned Smellfungus in *A Sentimental Journey.*

For recent books, *The Fall of Rome and the End of Civilization* (Oxford University Press, 2005), by **Bryan Ward-Perkins,** is a well-written account of the end of ancient Rome. There are of course innumerable scholarly books about Rome, including cradle-to-grave treatments of the empire's entire, nearly thousand-year history. The recent *The Romans: from Village to Empire* (Oxford, 2004) was written by three scholars and is supplemented with maps and illustrations, which go a long way toward making the history comprehensible.

For a good source of information on art and artists, we like **Karl Ludwig Gallwitz**'s *Handbook of Italian Renaissance Painters* (1999), a very user-friendly index that is especially good for understanding who collaborated with, taught, or influenced whom.

Fiction set in Rome is enormous. The granddaddy of historical fiction about Rome is Nobel Prize winner **Henryk Sienkiewicz**'s epic *Quo Vadis?,* first published in 1896 (reprint Hippocrene, 1999); set during the reign of Nero, it concerns a romantic plot about a love between a Christian woman and a Roman soldier. **Robert Graves**'s *I, Claudius* and *Claudius the God* (reprint Vintage, 1989), imaginary autobiographies of the emperor, are perennial favorites; Graves can be said to have created a subgenre. **Marguerite Yourcenar** wrote an exquisitely styled autobiography for a later emperor, Hadrian (*Memoirs of Hadrian;* reprint Farrar, Straus and Giroux 2005). If you are a mystery fan you might like to read **Lindsey Davis**'s series set in ancient Rome, or **Ian Pear**'s series on art theft capers.

Last but not least, there are the Italians themselves. **Alberto Moravia**'s *The Woman of Rome* (1949; Steerforth, 1999) is one of his best novels, set during the Fascist period and concerning a young girl and the men who struggle to control her.

Index